How to Not Be a Broke Pastor

The definitive guide for understanding AND maximizing the benefits from your pastoral compensation

S.L. POTTS

2018 Edition

Copyright © 2017 by BROKEPASTOR LLC.

All rights reserved. No part of this work may be reproduced, stored in a retrieval system, or transmitted in any form or by any means – electronic, mechanical, photocopy, recording, or otherwise – except for brief quotations for the purpose of review or comment, without the prior permission of the author.

Requests for information should be addressed to:
admin@brokepastor.com.

This publication is designed to provide competent and reliable information regarding the subject matter covered. However, it is sold with the understanding that the author and publisher are not engaged in rendering legal, accounting, financial, or other professional advice. Laws and practices often vary state to state and country to country, and if legal or other expert assistance is required, the services of a competent professional person should be sought. The author and publisher specifically disclaim any liability that is incurred from the use or application of the contents of this book. From a Declaration of Principles jointly adopted by a Committee of the American Bar Association and a Committee of Publishers and Associations.

Original and modified cover art by NaCDS and CoverDesignStudio.com.

Unless otherwise noted, Scripture quotations are from the ESV® Bible (The Holy Bible, English Standard Version®), copyright © 2001 by Crossway, a publishing ministry of Good News Publishers. Used by permission. All rights reserved.

ISBN-13: 978-0-9994737-4-0

Visit our website, www.brokepastor.com.

To my lovely wife, Jamie, who has stood by me through thick and thin, though richer or poorer, and has been my greatest earthly treasure.

TABLE OF CONTENTS

Chapter 1 - Our Story 13

SECTION 1

Chapter 2 - Understanding Taxes and SECA 21
    Not All Taxes are the Same 22
        Federal Income Tax 22
        Social Security Tax 23
        Medicare Tax 23
        State and Local Taxes 23
    Employment Status 24
        FICA vs. SECA 25
        Withholding Options 26
    Can My Church Pay SECA for Me? 27
    What Does All of This Mean for You? 27

Chapter 3 - Opting out of Social Security 31
    Social Security Exemption 32
        Parsing the Exemption 33
        What Did I Have to Consider? 35
    Exemption Requirements 36
    Time Limits for Exemption 37
    Miscellaneous Items 37
    What Does All of This Mean for You? 38

Chapter 4 - Salary vs Housing Allowance 41
    Pastoral Compensation 41
    Pastoral Income 42

| Salary | 42 |

Housing Allowance 43
   Technical Definition 43
   Practical Definition 43
   How does it work? 43
My Approach 47
Double Dipping 48
A Note on Tax Preparation Services and Software 49
What if I Live in a Parsonage? 50
How to Track Housing Expenses 51
What Does All of This Mean for You? 51

Chapter 5 - Benefits 53
  A General Principal 54
  Medical Insurance 55
  Vision/Dental Insurance 56
  Disability Insurance 57
  Paid Time Off (PTO) 58
  Planned Sabbaticals 59
  Retirement 60
  What Does All of This Mean for You? 60

Chapter 6 - Retirement 63
  SIMPLE IRA Accounts 64
  403(b) Accounts 65
  SEP IRA Accounts 66
  What Does All of This Mean for You? 67

Chapter 7 - Accountable Reimbursement Plans 69
  Non-Accountable Plans 70
  Accountable Plans 71
     You Have to Have a Plan 71
     Work-Related Expenses 71
     Types of Reimbursements 72
     Reimbursement Amounts 75
     Required Documentation 75
     Reporting/Retention Tools 75

Why I Love Reimbursable Plans 75
What Does All of This Mean for You? 76

Chapter 8 - Putting the Pieces Together 77
Making a Decision about Social Security 77
Balancing Salary and Housing Allowance 78
    Keeping Taxes in Mind 79
    Keeping Your Home in Mind 80
    Keeping Obamacare in Mind 81
    Keeping Retirement in Mind 81
    Finding the Right Balance 82
Balancing Cash Compensation Against Other Options 83
What Does All of This Mean for You? 85

SECTION 2

Chapter 9 - The Pastor's House 89
Your Greatest Financial Investment 91
What I Wish I Had Done 94

Chapter 10 - Pay Yourself Second 95
A Biblical Adjustment 95
A Three-Fold Approach 96
A Longer-Term Focus 97

Chapter 11 - Considering Your future 99
Expand Your Horizons 100
Consider Non-Pastoral Opportunities 101

Chapter 12 - Seeking Professional Help 103
Four Professionals Every Church Should Know 104
Don't Be the "Normal" Church 105

Chapter 13 - Final Thoughts 107

APPENDICES

Appendix A - Form 4361 Explanation Letter............................ 115

Appendix B - Next Steps 127

Chapter 1
Our Story

I'll never forget that phone call.

I was sitting in my study, working on Sunday's sermon, when the phone rang. It was my wife. She had driven with another lady in our church to go to a women's Bible study and had decided to stop at the bank to get $20 from the ATM.

For the very first time in our lives (before or since), we were overdrawn.

I had never experienced that feeling before – sickness and dread and fear all mingled together. To this day, I'm not sure what was worse – hearing the fear in her voice as she struggled to hold back the tears or the feeling of fear in my own heart as I was totally blindsided by the news.

How could this have happened?

As pastors, our time is very valuable. So, I'll get straight to the point: I want to help you avoid what my wife and I experienced that day.

I am writing this book because, while pastors may be very knowledgeable and capable when it comes to the Scriptures, to working with people, and to ministry . . . my experience is that far too many are completely clueless when it comes to their pastoral finances.

I know I was.

After four years of Bible college and four years of seminary, I became the lead pastor of a small, six-year-old church plant in September 2007. Even though the church was struggling in many ways, they wanted to do the best they could to help provide for us financially. They offered us a starting salary of $48,000/year along with full health coverage for our family.

The best part was, they said, that our salary would be "tax-free" because I was a pastor. We were so excited! We decided to buy a house based on that information. We set our budget based on that information. In fact, we planned a lot of things based on that information.

However, when I got my first monthly paycheck, instead of receiving $4,000, I received $3,388. Something called SECA had taken 15.3% of my expected salary away.

We were devastated.

There we were, less than one month into pastoral ministry, and our plans, our budget, and our house payment were all in serious jeopardy . . . and there was nothing we could do about it.

Now, before continuing, let me be clear about something. The church had neither lied to us nor purposefully misled us. Have you ever heard the old saying: "You don't know what you don't know"? Well, it's true for both pastors and churches.

The church didn't know enough about the unique intricacies of pastoral compensation to give us clear and accurate information. Technically, they were correct in saying that our salary would be "tax-free." It was. But it was not "SECA-free." And that distinction, or the lack thereof, took a 15.3% bite out of our paycheck and sent us into a financial tailspin.

Not only did the church not know these things, but I didn't either. I had spent the previous eight years of my life studying Greek, Hebrew, theology, church history, preaching, and pastoral ministry, but had never once been told a thing about understanding pastoral compensation. It wasn't that I had skipped that day of class. There was no class that taught these things.

And so . . . both I and the church were flying blind, totally unaware of what we didn't know. But what we didn't know was going to catch up to us quickly.

After assuring my wife that everything would be okay, I hung up the phone and just cried. For more than a year, I had been able to keep our budget somewhat on track by cutting every possible expense, using up all of our savings, and cashing in the small 401(k) I had gotten from a previous employer.

But we had now reached the end of those measures, and I had been caught off guard. I felt like such a failure.

As I sit here, over ten years later, and think back on these things, I am filled with a mix of both sadness and joy at the thought of them.

On the one hand, those are still painful memories for my wife and I, and even though God sustained us and provided for us through those times, there are pieces of our hearts that will likely always carry the scars of those days.

Yet, on the other hand, I can look back to those times and see the hand of God at work. By his grace, my family never went hungry. We were never homeless. In fact, after more than a decade of pastoral ministry, I can now see how God was using those things in our lives to not only better prepare us for ministry, but to also be a blessing to others. And for this, I am most joyful.

This is why I am writing.

I want to be a blessing to you and to prepare you for what <u>I wasn't prepared for</u>. It's often said that, in life, you can either do/learn things the easy way or the hard way. This is particularly true for pastors trying to understand and maximize the benefits from their compensation. I learned the hard way, but why should you?

In the chapters that follow, I will attempt to share with you what I, myself, have learned. I'm not going to share theory with you. I'm going to share my own experience.

Please know that I am not a lawyer. I am not an accountant. I am not a tax professional. I am not a financial planner. I'm just an average pastor of an average church who has spent ten years trying to understand the best way to be "wise as a serpent and innocent as a dove" when it comes to my pastoral compensation. **That said, before implementing any of the things discussed in this book, you should consult with and get counsel from the professionals listed above to ensure that you are doing and structuring things**

correctly, ethically, and within the bounds of the law. More on that in Chapter 12.

Three final thoughts, and we'll get started.

First, I've arranged this book in two main sections. In the first section, we'll consider some of the nuts and bolts of understanding pastoral compensation – from taxes to retirement and everything in between. Once we've laid a solid foundation, I'll suggest a few thoughts about how to put all of those pieces together into an actionable plan that will help you get the maximum benefit from your total compensation package.

In the second section, I'll address a few additional topics that I wish I had known about ten years ago that would have better prepared me to handle my pastoral finances wisely and to the benefit of my family.

Second, I have written two different versions of this book, one geared towards pastors – *How to Not Be a Broke Pastor* - and one geared towards church decision makers (i.e. Sessions, Elder boards, Deacon boards, Trustees, committees, congregations, etc.) – *Structuring Pastoral Compensation*. While there are similarities between the two books in terms of content, each covers topics specific to the audience at hand, and each is structured differently in terms of application.

If you are a pastor – particularly, if you are the lead pastor of your church, you should probably read both books so that you can understand both sides of the coin. But at the very least, you need to make sure that the people within your church who make decisions about pastoral compensation read *Structuring Pastoral Compensation*. More on that in Chapter 13.

Finally, after ten years of pastoring and of meeting other pastors, I've yet to meet a single one who has dedicated their life to vocational ministry for the purpose of getting rich. In fact, the more common experience is meeting pastors who, if they were in the secular workforce, would make much more money than they do as pastors.

None of us entered pastoral ministry to get rich, and this book is not intended to help you get rich - not in the slightest. If you feel that desire in your heart, see Paul's warning in 1 Timothy 6:6-10 and reconsider why you are reading this book!

My desire is not to help pastors get rich. As I said at the beginning, my sole desire is to be a blessing to you by sharing my own experience in the very unique world of pastoral compensation so that you can make wise financial decisions for yourself, your family, and your church . . . and thus be a blessing to others.

May God use these feeble words in ways I would never dream or imagine.

SECTION 1

Chapter 2
Understanding Taxes and SECA

"Therefore, render to Caesar the things that are Caesar's, and to God the things that are God's."

-Matthew 22:21-

• • •

So, let's go back to what I was told by our church when they first informed me about my salary ten years ago. They said that I would receive $48,000/year "tax-free." Was this statement true or false?

The answer is: YES!

If you are a pastor of an average-sized church in America receiving an average-sized pastoral income, generally speaking, all income that you will receive for your duties in the ministry will very likely be free from income tax.

However, while this statement is technically true, there are a number of things which impact how this actually works on Tax Day.

Not All Taxes are the Same

People often tend to think of taxes as the lump sum of all money taken out of their paycheck before they get it. When people complain about taxes, they usually don't make any distinction between the multiple components of taxation that each worker pays. However, it is important to understand the four main components.

Federal Income Tax

This is the amount that actually goes toward paying the taxes you owe based on your income level and claimed deductions. This amount is affected by the number of personal allowances you take when you fill out your W4, and it is also the amount that you can possibly get a refund on when you file your 1040 at the end of the year.

As pastors, we only pay federal income taxes on our salary, and not on our housing allowance.[1]

As stated earlier, if you are an average pastor of an average-sized church in America who receives your pastoral income in an average way, you will likely (for the most part) be completely free from federal income taxes. Of course, this depends somewhat on your situation and salary level. If you become the pastor of a large and generous church that pays you $250,000/year, then you may likely pay federal income taxes on at least some portion of your salary.

Regardless of whether or not you have to pay income taxes, it is important to note that there is no official exemption from paying federal income tax for pastors (or anyone else for that matter).

---

[1] See Chapter 4 for more information.

Social Security Tax
Social Security Tax makes up the majority of what is often referred to as FICA.[2] FICA taxes are collected at a rate of 7.65% on gross income up to $127,200 in 2017 for non-ministerial employees. Of that 7.65%, 6.2% goes towards Social Security.

As pastors, we must pay Social Security taxes on both our salary and our housing allowance, but we can file for an official exemption from paying Social Security tax by submitting Form 4361 in a timely manner.[3]

Medicare Tax
Medicare Tax makes up the remainder of FICA at 1.45% of gross income for non-ministerial employees.

As pastors, we must pay Medicare taxes on both our salary and our housing allowance, but we can file for an official exemption from paying Medicare tax by submitting Form 4361 in a timely manner.[4]

State and Local Taxes
Obviously, laws regarding ministerial income and state/local taxes vary by state. You will need to ask a local accountant or tax professional about any special tax issues related to ministerial income in your state of residence. Having said that, generally speaking, if you are free from paying federal income taxes, you may possibly be free from paying state income taxes as well.

---

[2] See FICA vs. SECA below for more information.

[3] See Chapter 3.

[4] Again, see Chapter 3.

Employment Status

A second thing you need to understand about how taxes affect pastoral compensation is your employment status. Your employment status in a secular job is crystal clear: you are either self-employed or you are an employee of someone else. Unfortunately, for pastors, the issue of employment status is not so clear-cut.

IRS Tax Topic 417 (Earnings for Clergy) will illustrate the complexity of this issue:

> A licensed, commissioned, or ordained minister is generally the common law employee of the church, denomination, sect, or organization that employs him or her to provide ministerial services. However, there are some exceptions, such as traveling evangelists who are independent contractors (self-employed) under the common law. If you're a minister performing ministerial services, all of your earnings, including wages, offerings, and fees you receive for performing marriages, baptisms, funerals, etc., are subject to income tax, whether you earn the amount as an employee or self-employed person. However, how you treat expenses related to those earnings differs if you earn the income as an employee or as a self-employed person.
>
> For social security and Medicare tax purposes, regardless of your status under the common law, the services you perform in the exercise of your ministry are considered self-employment earnings and are generally subject to self-employment tax. See Publication 517, *Social Security and Other*

Information for Members of the Clergy and Religious Workers, for limited exceptions from self-employment tax.[5]

If you can translate and understand ancient Hebrew texts with ease, but feel incapable of translating and understanding IRS regulations, here is what this means: **most pastors will be treated BOTH as an employee and as a self-employed contractor at the same time and for the same job by the IRS**. Or, to put it in a more commonly used term, pastors are considered "dual-status employees."

Now, this isn't always the case, and you will need to clarify your employment status as soon as possible in the early days of your ministry. Some pastors choose to act and be treated as a self-employed contractor across the board (though, I think this is rare).

Normally, you will be considered an employee of the church for federal income tax purposes and a self-employed contractor for Social Security and Medicare purposes. This distinction is important to understand because of the differences between FICA and SECA and because of how it affects your withholdings for your ministerial pay.

FICA vs. SECA
What is the difference between FICA and SECA? FICA is an acronym for the Federal Insurance Contributions Act. SECA is an acronym for the Self-Employment Contributions Act. Both do the same thing – they extract money from your paycheck to cover Social Security and Medicare taxes.

---

[5] https://www.irs.gov/taxtopics/tc417.html.

However, even though they do the same thing, the differences they make on a pastor's paycheck can be significant.

Under FICA, you and your employer split the cost of coverage 50/50. You pay 7.65% out of your gross income, and your employer pays a matching amount out of their own pocket for a grand total payment equal to 15.3% of your gross annual income. So, for example, if you make $50,000/year, you will pay $3,825 in FICA taxes, and your employer will pay an additional $3,825 in FICA taxes for a total FICA payment of $7,650. However, because you only paid half of that amount, your net income for the year would be $46,175 (not including income taxes or any other deductions).

But if you are self-employed, you don't have an employer to pay that other half. Does the government just allow self-employed individuals to pay half? No. Under SECA, you pay the full cost of your Social Security and Medicare tax, yourself... 15.3%! Again, for example, let's say that you make $50,000/year in self-employment income. Under SECA, you will have to pay the full $7,650 yourself – leaving you with $42,350 in net income (not including income taxes or any other deductions).

Under SECA, allowances are made to help balance the differences from FICA (to a point), but in the end, you will likely be paying a large portion of your salary into SECA. While your ministerial income may be, effectively, free from federal income taxes, it is not free from SECA unless you file for an exemption.

Withholding Options
Another area where your employment status matters is in the issue of paycheck withholdings. As an employee of a secular company, your payroll department deducts the proper amount of federal and state

income taxes, as well as FICA payments, from each paycheck automatically. They then turn that money over to the IRS to be "credited to your account."

People who are self-employed have to do that for themselves (or pay an accountant to do it for them) and must send their payments to the IRS on, at least, a quarterly basis.

Because pastors are considered to be both employees and self-employed contractors, the proper way to handle their withholdings is a bit unusual, and you should check with an accountant or tax professional to get guidance on how best to manage this in your specific circumstance.

Can My Church Pay SECA for Me?

No. And the reason why should now be clear – it's because the IRS considers you to be self-employed . . . from the perspective of SECA. The only thing your church can likely do is "gross up" your income in order to get your net income where they want it.[6]

What Does All of This Mean for You?

Now that we have the facts, let's bring all of this together and make it as simple and clear as we can.

Because the overwhelming majority of pastors are viewed by the IRS as being dual-status employees (i.e. employee AND self-employed), your income will be treated by the IRS in two completely different ways.

---

[6] However, raising your income like that could have other negative impacts. See Chapter 8 for more details.

From the perspective of federal income tax (the first line deducted from your paycheck), the IRS will only look at your salary and NOT your housing allowance and/or parsonage.[7]

However, from the perspective of SECA (the second and third lines deducted from your paycheck), the IRS will look at both your salary AND your housing allowance and/or parsonage.

As an example, Pastor Bob receives $50,000/year in income from his church. Of that $50,000, he takes $25,000 as salary and $25,000 as housing allowance. Since the IRS will only collect income tax on his salary, his taxable income is only $25,000, not $50,000.

But wait! That's before his standard and/or itemized deductions. If Pastor Bob has a wife and two kids and if he owns his own home, those deductions alone will likely reduce his taxable income to almost (or probably below) $0. From the perspective of his federal income taxes, he is "tax-free"!

What about SECA? Remember, from the perspective of SECA, the IRS looks at both his salary and his housing allowance . . . which means that he will have to pay 15.3% of his $50,000 income to cover those payments alone. That totals $7,650!

---

[7] If you do not understand the difference between income, salary, and housing allowance, the following equation will help: pastoral income = salary + housing allowance. For the reason why this distinction is important, see Chapter 4. Also, I think that the idea of a parsonage has to be one of the very worst ideas ever developed by churches. For why this is so, again, see Chapter 4.

All of sudden, Pastor Bob's $50,000/year income just became $42,350/year.

In Pastor Bob's case, if his church really wanted him to take home (or net) $50,000/year, they would have to pay him $60,000/year to make sure SECA didn't take him below that number.[8]

Again, it's a bit more involved than this, but now you can see why these things matter so much! This is what I had to learn the hard way.

---

[8] 15.3% of $60,000 is $9,180 – leaving Pastor Bob with a net income of $50,820.

Chapter 3
Opting out of Social Security

"Pray for us, for we are sure that we have a clear conscience, desiring to act honorably in all things."

-Hebrews 13:18-

• • •

After weeks of wrestling with the decision, I finally put the letter in the mail – I was opting out of Social Security. There was no sense of excitement on my part. Actually, I was quite scared. Had I made the right decision? Had my motivations been right? Was I being honest with myself, my church, and the government? These were weighty questions, and ones that I took very seriously.

In the previous chapter, I made reference to the fact that pastors <u>cannot</u> file for an official exemption from paying federal income taxes, but <u>can</u> file for an official exemption from paying Social Security and Medicare taxes (better known as SECA) by submitting Form 4361 in a timely manner.

It has been my observation that there is a great deal of misunderstanding among pastors regarding this - not to mention among well-meaning, but ill-informed church members. Let's see if we can clear things up a bit.

SOCIAL SECURITY EXEMPTION

The only way most pastors can avoid paying SECA is to file for an official exemption from paying such taxes with the IRS. While this may sound attractive at first, it requires much thought and honesty on the part of the pastor.

In order to become exempt from SECA, pastors must file Form 4361 (titled, "Application for Exemption From Self-Employment Tax for Use by Ministers, Members of Religious Orders and Christian Science Practitioners") affirming the following statement:

> I certify that I am conscientiously opposed to, or because of my religious principles I am opposed to, the acceptance (for services I perform as a minister, member of a religious order not under a vow of poverty, or a Christian Science practitioner) of any public insurance that makes payments in the event of death, disability, old age, or retirement; or that makes payments toward the cost of, or provides services for, medical care. (Public insurance includes insurance systems established by the Social Security Act.)

> I certify that as a duly ordained, commissioned, or licensed minister of a church or a member of a religious order not under a vow of poverty, I have informed the ordaining, commissioning, or licensing body of my church or order that I am conscientiously opposed to, or because of religious principles, I am opposed to the acceptance (for services I perform as a minister or as a member of a religious order) of any public insurance that makes payments in the event of

death, disability, old age, or retirement; or that makes payments toward the cost of, or provides services for, medical care, including the benefits of any insurance system established by the Social Security Act.

I certify that I have never filed Form 2031 to revoke a previous exemption from social security coverage on earnings as a minister, member of a religious order not under a vow of poverty, or a Christian Science practitioner.

I request to be exempted from paying self-employment tax on my earnings from services as a minister, member of a religious order not under a vow of poverty, or a Christian Science practitioner, under section 1402(e) of the Internal Revenue Code. I understand that the exemption, if granted, will apply only to these earnings. Under penalties of perjury, I declare that I have examined this application and to the best of my knowledge and belief, it is true and correct.[9]

What does that mean?

Parsing the Exemption
"I certify that I am conscientiously opposed to, or because of my religious principles I am opposed to . . ."

What this means is that pastors must have an honest, religiously-based objection to contributing to Social Security or Medicare out of their ministerial income. Financial/political/personal objections do not

---

[9] https://www.irs.gov/pub/irs-pdf/f4361.pdf.

count and cannot be honestly used. Your objection must be based on either your conscience or on some Biblical principle.

". . . the acceptance (for services I perform as a minister, member of a religious order not under a vow of poverty, or a Christian Science practitioner) of any public insurance . . ."

In my opinion, this is the most important segment in the entire affirmation.

Please note that this is regarding "public insurance," not income taxes. In other words, this is about entitlement programs, not supporting the government through normal taxation. Income taxes support the state. FICA and SECA fund entitlement programs. It is money taken from you now so that it can be given back to you at a later date.

Notice, secondly, that it is about the "acceptance" of public insurance, not necessarily payments towards public insurance that you are saying you are opposed to. Some people draw a major distinction between those two things, but I think that is a false dichotomy. The government has set up no system for paying into public insurance without receiving payments back, or for receiving payments out of it without first paying into it. Therefore, since "acceptance" of public insurance necessitates payments into it, I would see the two as one.

Third, notice that it is specifically targeted at the acceptance of public insurance "for service I perform as a minister." This is talking about your pastoral duties only. It is not talking about secular employment, or non-pastoral duties. Later in the statement, this idea is confirmed and clarified when it says, "I understand that the exemption, if granted, will apply only to these earnings."

Therefore, I came to realize that this was not asking me whether or not I was opposed to paying taxes, nor was it asking me whether or not I was opposed to public insurance (i.e. Social Security, Medicare, etc.) as a general principle.

What it was asking me was whether or not I had a religious objection to having 15.3% of my gross pay that I received from my pastoral duties given to the government so that they could give it back to me later. That was the question I had to wrestle with in deciding if I should file Form 4361.

What Did I Have to Consider?
Once I understood the question being asked, I began to ask new questions of myself.

What was the true motivation of my heart? We are all willing to quote Jeremiah 17:9[10] when it fits in a sermon, but was I equally willing to apply it to myself when 15.3% of my annual income was on the line?

What were my true beliefs regarding the separation of church and state? Many pastors say that they believe in the separation of church and state, but what does that really mean in practice?

What was my theology/philosophy of pastoral compensation? What does the Bible say about the pastor's salary? Whose responsibility is it to provide for the pastor?

---

[10] "The heart is deceitful above all things, and desperately sick; who can understand it?"

If you were to consider opting out of Social Security, I would assume that you may need to consider these same questions as well.

Exemption Requirements

According to the IRS, if you choose to apply for exemption, you will need to do the following things:

1. Print out Form 4361 from the IRS website.
2. Fill out section one with your name, address, SSN, and telephone number.
3. Fill out section two by marking your correct classification.
4. Fill out section three by entering the date you were licensed/ordained/etc.
5. Make a copy of your licensing/ordination certificate to be included with the application.
6. Fill out section four with your church's name, address, and employer identification number (can be found on your W2).
7. Fill out section five by listing the first two years that you received pay for religious services in excess of $400 (see Time Limits for Exemption below).
8. Fill out section six (if applicable) by explaining the difference between how your church views licensed and ordained ministers.
9. Fill out section seven by signing and dating that you are in agreement with the statement listed above.
10. Make two copies of the signed and completed Form 4361 to be included along with the original application and other supporting documents.
11. Mail all items to the IRS.
12. Inform your church that you have applied for exemption.

13. Allow 8-12 weeks for a response.[11]

TIME LIMITS FOR EXEMPTION

According to the instructions on Form 4361, you must "file Form 4361 by the due date, including extensions, of your tax return for the 2nd tax year in which you had at least $400 of net earnings from self-employment, any of which came from services performed as a minister, member of a religious order, or Christian Science practitioner."[12] Again, what does this mean?

Let's say that Pastor Bob becomes the pastor of Faith Church on January 1, 2017. Assuming this is his first pastorate (and, more importantly, his first time receiving income for his ministerial duties), he has until April 15, 2019, to file for an exemption from SECA.

Across town, Pastor George becomes the pastor of Grace Church on December 15, 2017. Assuming this is his first pastorate (and, more importantly, his first time receiving income for his ministerial duties), he also has until April 15, 2019, to file for an exemption if he earns at least $400 from his pastoral duties in those sixteen days. If he does not, he would have until April 15, 2020.

MISCELLANEOUS ITEMS

If you choose to file for an exemption after having already paid SECA taxes for your services in the ministry, you may have the right to file for a refund of those withholdings. In order to get your refund, you will likely need to file an amended return for each tax year in which you paid into SECA for your ministerial services.

---

[11] https://www.irs.gov/pub/irs-pdf/p517.pdf.
[12] https://www.irs.gov/pub/irs-pdf/f4361.pdf.

If you have already paid into Social Security via FICA (e.g. through previously held secular employment) and have earned credits toward retirement, it is likely that you will not lose those credits even if you file for an exemption from SECA.

If you are bi-vocational, you should continue to pay FICA taxes on your secular income regardless of whether or not you are exempt from paying SECA taxes for your ministerial income.

There have been periods where the government has opened the door to allow pastors who had previously opted out of Social Security to opt back in (the most recent, I believe, being under President Clinton from 1999-2002). This option may or may not come up again in the future.

Ministers are the only people who get to opt out of paying Social Security taxes. Please recognize that this choice may not always exist.

WHAT DOES ALL OF THIS MEAN FOR YOU?
It means that you have a decision to make, and that you don't have a lot of time to make it.

If you have already been a pastor for two years, and you did not opt out of SECA, it would seem that your deadline has likely passed. Unless something changes, you likely cannot opt out.

But if you are new to pastoral ministry, you will have to make your own decision in regard to whether or not you opt out before your second tax filing as a pastor. No one can make this decision for you.

As I said at the beginning, I opted out. I did not arrive at that decision lightly, and I recognize that it is not for everyone. Two of my dearest friends in ministry made the opposite decision, and they did not arrive at that decision lightly either.

Just by way of illustration, I have included the letter of explanation that I sent to the IRS and to our Elder Board when I submitted my Form 4361.[13] I am not suggesting that this is what you should do, nor am I saying that my reasons should be yours. I am just giving it to you so that you can see where my mind and heart were at the time I applied for exemption.

Keep in mind that there are legitimate financial pros and cons to either opting out or staying in. However, since your decision cannot be based on financial reasons, it behooves you and your integrity to put those thoughts out of your mind as much as possible.

May God grant you honesty, integrity, and grace as you wrestle through this very difficult decision.

---

[13] See Appendix A.

CHAPTER 4
SALARY VS HOUSING ALLOWANCE

"You shall not muzzle an ox when it is treading out the grain."

-Deuteronomy 25:4-

• • •

Of all the components of my pastoral income that I strategize over year after year, none is more important to me than the balance between my salary and my housing allowance. This one area touches almost every other piece of my compensation, and I cannot stress to you how critical it is to understand and utilize this properly.

Let's start by defining a few terms.

PASTORAL COMPENSATION
When I talk about pastoral compensation, I am referring to the totality of a pastor's income and all employee benefits which he receives. These things are, obviously, either decided upon by the church at the time he is hired, or developed over time as the church's ability to provide them for its pastor grows.

Pastoral Income

For the purposes of this book, pastoral income is the combination of a pastor's base salary and his housing allowance. Your church is responsible for setting the overall amount of your income, but only you can determine what amount of that income will be designated as salary and what amount will be designated as housing allowance.[14]

Salary

The amount of your income that you do not designate as housing allowance is automatically designated as salary. For example, if your pastoral income is set at $50,000/year, and you designate $30,000 as housing allowance, then your salary for that year is automatically $20,000.

Remember, your salary is the only portion of your income that is considered taxable for federal income tax purposes. That doesn't mean that you want that number to be as small as possible. In fact, my experience has shown that making it too small can actually work against you.[15]

---

[14] This is practically correct, but technically incorrect. Technically, a pastor is supposed to submit a designation request of some sort to the church indicating how much of his income he wants to be designated as housing allowance. The church (or a governing body within the church) must then approve that designation. However, practically speaking, it has been my observation that churches usually approve whatever is submitted by the pastor since the pastor alone will be accountable for that designation at tax time.

[15] See Chapter 8.

Housing Allowance

In my opinion, the most important tax benefit that pastors get to take advantage of is that of the housing allowance. Because it is so vitally important, let's break this down into a few bite-sized pieces.

Technical Definition

What is the housing allowance? Here is the definition from the Internal Revenue Code (IRC), Section 107: "In the case of a minister of the gospel, gross income does not include – (1) the rental value of a home furnished to him as part of his compensation; or (2) the rental allowance paid to him as a part of his compensation, to the extent used by him to rent or provide a home and to the extent such allowance does not exceed the fair rental value of the home, including furnishings and appurtenances such as a garage, plus the cost of utilities."[16]

Practical Definition

So, what is Section 107 talking about? It is explaining that pastors are allowed to designate a portion of their income to be used for the payment of housing-related expenses, and that this amount will not be counted as salary for federal income tax purposes (dependent on the details below).

How does it work?

At the beginning of each fiscal year, before you receive your first paycheck, you can elect to designate a portion of your annual salary towards your housing allowance. This amount should be excluded (not

---

[16] https://www.gpo.gov/fdsys/pkg/USCODE-2011-title26/pdf/USCODE-2011-title26-subtitleA-chap1-subchapB-partIII-sec107.pdf.

deducted) from your gross income on your W2 and 1040 for income tax purposes.

While you can designate any percentage or amount of your annual income as being your housing allowance, when you actually file your taxes, you will be required to "claim" the dollar amount that represents the least of the following three options:

1. The amount actually designated as housing allowance.
2. The amount actually spent on housing-related expenses.
3. The amount of the fair-market rental value of a pastor's home, fully furnished, with utilities.

Think through these three options.

The amount actually designated as housing allowance refers to the amount of your income that you designate/request as being set aside for housing allowance at the beginning of the fiscal year. If you make $50,000/year and you designate $25,000 of that amount as being housing allowance, then $25,000 is your designation.

The amount actually spent on housing-related expenses refers to what you actually spend throughout the year on your home.

The good news here is that most reasonable household expenses can be included. For example: a down payment on a home, mortgage payments (including both interest and principal), home equity loan payments (assuming the loan proceeds are used for housing-related expenses), real estate taxes, property insurance, mortgage insurance, utilities, furnishings and appliances (including repairs), structural or cosmetic repairs and improvements, remodeling, yard maintenance and improvements, pest control, snow removal, general maintenance items, trash pickup, and even household cleaning supplies. As you can see, there are a lot of options here![17]

So, for example, let's say that, at the end of the year, you add up all of your housing-related expenses and find that you actually spent a total of $22,540. That would be your actual housing-related expense total.

The amount of the fair-market rental value of your home, fully furnished, with utilities refers to . . . well, exactly what it says. If you were going to rent out your home at a fair-market price in your area, how much would you be able to charge in rent per month? In addition, how much do you spend on all utilities throughout the year? Whatever that total number is, divide it by twelve, and that's how much you would have to charge for utilities per month.

While those numbers shouldn't be too hard to figure out, notice that the requirement is for the "fair-market rental value of your home, <u>fully furnished</u>, with utilities." Now, depending on where you live, that may not be too hard to figure out. But for many pastors, especially those in rural or suburban settings, this is nearly impossible to objectively determine because very few people rent fully furnished homes anymore. So, how do we determine the rental value of our furnishings?

Unfortunately, the IRS provides us with no guidance on how to arrive at this number. What, then, should we do? Well, based on years of trying to find the best answer to this singular question, what I have decided to do is to choose a number/formula that seems reasonable

---

[17] Just to be clear, housing-related expenses can only be included in the housing allowance for the year in which they are incurred. They cannot be carried over to a future year, nor used in advance.

to me based on our area, our home, and the quality and quantity of our furnishings, and then stick with that number/formula every year, with only modest increases to account for inflation.

By way of example only, let's say that, in your neighborhood, the fair-market rental value of your home is $1,000/month. Given the area you live in, the quality of your home, and both the quality and quantity of your furnishings, you decide on a furnishings value formula equal to 20% of monthly rent . . . or $200/month. Add in the average cost of your monthly utilities (let's say $300/month), and you now have a grand total fair-market rental value of your home, fully furnished, with utilities of $1,500/month or $18,000/year.[18]

If all of this seems far too subjective to you, you're in good company. However, without clear guidance from the IRS, this kind of approach is likely the best you can do.

Before moving on, let me say one more thing about fair-market rental value. Since there is no single formula or approach I can give you that will make this easy or clear, the danger is that we either A) short-change ourselves by arriving at a number that is too low, or B) exaggerate this number to something outrageously and unjustifiably high. The former hurts you unnecessarily, and the latter is just plain dishonest. Please avoid both extremes.[19]

---

[18] Please know that I am not suggesting the 20% formula as being a good "rule-of-thumb" for calculating this number. There is just too much ambiguity on this point for any single formula, number, or approach to be viewed as standard or normative. This is merely an example.

[19] In all likelihood, problem A is a bigger danger than problem B for most pastors. Just know that underestimation does not equal godliness.

Why don't we compare these three numbers using our old friend, Pastor Bob? Let's say that Pastor Bob is given an income of $50,000/year and designates $25,000 as housing allowance. At tax time, after adding up all of his housing expenses, he realizes that he only spent $22,540 on his home. However, when he calculates the fair-market rental value of his home, fully furnished, with utilities, he realizes it is only worth $18,000/year. Since he can only claim the least of these three numbers as being his housing allowance for the previous fiscal year, that means that he can only claim $18,000 as housing allowance, and that the rest of his income ($32,000) will be treated as taxable salary on his 1040.

Let's try this example again, but with a few changes. Like last time, Pastor Bob has an income of $50,000/year and designates $25,000 of that as housing allowance. At tax time, after adding up all of his housing expenses, he finds that he spent $26,540 on his home. In addition, when he calculates the fair-market rental value of his home, fully furnished, with utilities, he realizes that it is worth $28,500/year. Since the least of these three numbers is $25,000, that is all he can claim as housing allowance on his 1040. The rest of his income will be treated as taxable salary.

Do you get the idea?

My Approach
Given these facts, what I have decided to do is to calculate the fair-market rental value of my home, fully furnished, with utilities before I designate my housing allowance each year ... and then I designate <u>that exact same amount</u> as being my housing allowance for the coming year.

For example, if I determine that my fair-market rental valuation is $25,000, then I designate $25,000 as being my housing allowance. If it's $30,000, then I designate $30,000. Since it has to be the least of the three numbers, I don't see any point in making one of these two numbers higher than the other because, then, the lower number automatically wins.

In our case, there is a logical and reasonable spectrum of fair-market rental value for our home with our furnishings in our area, and I purposefully choose the upper end of that spectrum each year. It's not outrageous, but neither is it too low. I then choose that exact same amount as being my designated housing allowance for the coming year.

Approaching it this way means that the only "wild card" left in the equation is my actual housing expenses for the fiscal year . . . and, at least . . . hopefully . . . I will have some control over that!

I can choose to spend the full amount of my designation (or even over it), thereby maximizing my housing allowance benefit, or I can choose to spend less than my designation and thereby increase my taxable income.[20] Again, at least in theory, I'm in control of that decision.

Double Dipping

Here is what makes the pastor's housing allowance even more of a blessing. Despite the fact that your housing allowance is excluded from your pastoral income for income tax purposes, you can normally still deduct your mortgage interest from your remaining, non-housing allowance income the same way any other tax filer can. I call this "double dipping."

---

[20] I'll explain why this may be desirable in Chapter 8.

For example, if you make $50,000/year and claim $25,000 as your housing allowance on your 1040, you will only be required to pay income taxes on the remaining $25,000. But, if you paid $10,000 in mortgage interest, you should be able to deduct that amount from your remaining income to end up with only $15,000 in taxable income (apart from other deductions). As with the ability to opt out of Social Security and Medicare taxes, you should recognize that this opportunity may not always exist.[21]

A Note on Tax Preparation Services and Software
I have heard from many pastors that the majority of tax preparers and tax preparation services that they have worked with in the past are inexperienced when it comes to understanding and properly handling the unique issues surrounding the pastor's income and, in particular, housing allowance.

I would suggest that, if you choose to use an individual or a service to prepare your taxes, make sure that the specific person you will be working with has experience with pastoral tax issues. If you're having a hard time finding someone like that, ask other local pastors for recommendations.

If you're more of a DIY kind of tax filer, and you want to utilize one of the major online tax software options, I would recommend contacting them in advance to ensure that their software is designed to process clergy taxes without problems.

---

[21] Over the past several years, the Freedom from Religion Foundation has been repeatedly suing the federal government in an attempt to get this particular provision of the tax code ruled unconstitutional. Should they succeed, the repercussions for pastors would be far-reaching.

For example, and to my knowledge, as of the 2016 tax filing season, TurboTax® may have been one of the few major online tax services capable of fully handling clergy taxes without any issues for DIY filers.[22] I know other pastors who attempted to use other major online tax services to file their clergy taxes, but who were unable to do so for various reasons.

WHAT IF I LIVE IN A PARSONAGE?
This is one scenario where I believe the kindness of your church may, almost certainly, work against you. If you live in a church-provided home, then you may or may not be allowed to exclude anything from your salary. If you can't, whatever you get is what you get.

That would be okay if it wasn't for the way SECA is counted when a parsonage is involved. Section 107 of the IRC requires pastors to pay SECA on their salary AND the fair-market rental value of any home furnished to them as part of their compensation (i.e. a parsonage).

Let's say you make $25,000/year and live in a parsonage with a fair-market rental value of $25,000. For income tax purposes, you will only be taxed on $25,000. But for SECA purposes, you will likely be taxed at 15.3% on $50,000. That means that you would only net $17,350!

So, not only could you have to give up a larger percentage of your actual income in SECA taxes, but you also don't get the benefit of building equity in a home of your own that you could recoup later.

In my humble (or not so humble) opinion, a parsonage is just about the worst thing a church could give to its pastor.

---

[22] TurboTax® is not a sponsor of this book.

How to Track Housing Expenses

Every January, I create a file in my filing cabinet for that year's tax-related documents. In this file, I put any and all home-related receipts, bills, and invoices. I mean ALL of them: every receipt; every utility bill; absolutely anything and everything that can be counted as an expense for our home goes into that file. This way, when I file my taxes the following February, I can find everything in one convenient location.

What Does All of This Mean for You?

It means that you are going to have to think carefully about how you want to manage this amazing tax benefit. In Chapter 8, I will give you a few ideas about how your housing allowance can be used in conjunction with the other items discussed in Chapters 2-7.

That said, the most obvious way to use your housing allowance is to pay for and improve your own home. In Chapter 9, we'll consider just how important this is.

Chapter 5
Benefits

"Every good gift and every perfect gift is from above, coming down from the Father of lights, with whom there is no variation or shadow due to change."

-James 1:17-

• • •

For years, the only benefits I received from our church were health/dental insurance and an undefined amount of vacation leave (which I rarely took in those early years for various reasons). I did not receive vision insurance . . . or disability coverage . . . or any retirement benefits. You get the picture.

This was particularly hard for us because I had come from the secular workforce where all of those things were provided for me (almost) from day one. And while it took me a few years to really begin missing them, the loss of those benefits eventually took their toll.

Whether you are currently in a pastorate or are on the verge of getting started, I cannot stress to you enough how important it is for you to give serious thought to the issue of your benefits package.

Now, even as I write these words, I recognize that there is a certain amount of this that is not in your control. For example, your church may be part of a denomination that provides a set package of benefits to all the pastors within your denomination. Or, maybe your church isn't a part of a denomination, but due to its size and budget, your church is very limited as to what it can provide to you by way of benefits.

My goal in this chapter is not to make "the perfect the enemy of the good," nor is it to make you discontent with whatever God has provided for you through your church. My goal is simply to make sure that you're thinking about the types of benefits that either should be or could be offered in order to be a blessing to you.[23]

A GENERAL PRINCIPAL

I have a philosophy that guides my thinking in relation to church employee compensation and benefits. Before I share it, notice that I included all church employees, not just pastors. This applies to any and every employee a church may hire. Here is my guiding philosophy for church employees:

---

[23] This chapter is one of the main reasons why I have written a companion guide to this book specifically for church decision makers titled *Structuring Pastoral Compensation: A Practical Guide for Blessing Your Pastor*. At the risk of sounding like a shameless salesman, I think you should consider buying a copy of that book for every Elder, Deacon, Trustee, or other leader within your church who makes decisions about pastoral compensation so that they can be aware of the very issues we are discussing here . . . particularly the issue of benefits. Remember, like you, they don't know what they don't know.

The church of Jesus Christ should attempt to treat its employees as well as, if not better than, the best secular employers of our day.

I can hear the cynic respond, "Of course you'd say that! You've got a dog in the fight." Well, you are correct. I do have a dog in the fight, but this philosophy is not driven by my own current employment status, but rather by my belief that the church is to be a city on a hill - a light in a very dark world - in every single aspect of its life and dealings before this broken world. And this can be nowhere more vividly and practically displayed than in the realm of employee care.

I grew up in circles where pastors and Christian workers of all types were viewed as having, effectively, taken a vow of poverty as a condition of their employment. I can think of dozens of faithful, Christian school teachers, for example, who were paid poverty-level wages (or likely below) in exchange for their service.

Even for pastors, too many churches act as if it is okay to give little, if any, thought to truly being a blessing to those whose responsibility it is to shepherd their souls.

This just should not be!

While my philosophy may be an ideal that few, if any, churches or ministries ever fully attain, it should at least be the guiding force behind every decision that is made. With this being my philosophy, here are a few thoughts on five main areas of employment benefits for pastors.

MEDICAL INSURANCE

Pastors should be provided with adequate medical insurance coverage for themselves and their families. Since premiums paid by the church on behalf of an employee are not, usually, considered taxable income,

I believe very strongly that churches should pay the full cost of a pastor's medical insurance coverage so as to reduce any taxable income for the pastor.

Now, I would be negligent if I didn't mention the 800-pound gorilla in the room – Obamacare. Regardless of your personal or political views on the issue, the Affordable Care Act has become a real problem for many pastors and churches.

However, if viewed from the right perspective, I believe that Obamacare could actually be one of the best things that has ever happened to either pastors or churches.

While it is beyond the scope of this book to really develop this topic, I have written a small book available on Amazon and at my website (www.brokepastor.com) that will help you think through the ways churches and pastors may be able to benefit from the ACA.[24]

Regardless of how the insurance is provided, I believe that this is the most important benefit a church can provide for its pastor.

Vision/Dental Insurance
Along with medical insurance, every pastor should be provided with vision and dental insurance. Neither of these coverages are generally included in most medical insurance plans for adults, and as such, both areas need to be supplemented with these additional coverages.

---

[24] *Benefitting from Obamacare* is the true story of how our church used the provisions of the ACA to save more than $100,000 in medical insurance premiums over the past three years while, at the same time, providing the best medical insurance possible for our pastoral staff.

There are many, many options for providing vision and dental coverage (both within and apart from Obamacare), and churches can choose the best option for the pastor and his family.

Disability Insurance

While fairly standard in the secular workplace, disability insurance coverage does not seem to be as common amongst pastors and churches. Yet, the possibility of a pastor becoming disabled is no less than any other worker in any other profession, and churches should be ready to care for any pastor who becomes disabled - either directly or through the purchase of disability coverage.

Notice the two options I just gave for caring for a disabled pastor.[25] One option is for the church to care for a pastor who becomes disabled *directly* – meaning, the church is willing and able to keep that pastor on its payroll (at some level or another) indefinitely, regardless of work performed or services rendered. While this may save the church money on annual premium payments now, it places all of the long-term risk on the church – a commitment that may or may not be feasible in the present or future.

The second option - and the one I would highly recommend - for caring for a pastor who becomes disabled is through the purchase of disability insurance coverage. Yes, the church will incur an expense related to the annual premiums, but this is generally minimal – especially when you compare it to the idea of keeping a pastor on your payroll indefinitely should they become disabled. This way, the church

---

[25] I'm assuming that a church not providing care for a disabled pastor isn't one of their options. How unloving, uncaring, and un-Christlike would that be?

transfers the long-term risk to the insurance provider, and everyone can have peace-of-mind knowing that the pastor will be cared for should the unthinkable happen.

PAID TIME OFF (PTO)

Pastors should be given a generous amount of paid vacation or personal leave time. While in seminary, I worked in the credit card and, later, mortgage departments of an international bank. Within three months of my employment, I was already receiving 18 days of PTO every calendar year (not including holidays). This wasn't because I was special in any way. It was just their standard policy for all employees. That was three-and-a-half weeks of paid vacation! By the time I left, I was entitled to 23 days of PTO – nearly five weeks!

Now, think about that from this perspective: that was for a job that never once called me in the middle of the night because of an emergency; that never once had me in tears over someone's pain or sinful choices; that never once asked me to stand at the bedside of a dear friend and fellow pastor to watch him take his last breath; and that never once was going to require me to answer for the souls of the people we served.

If there was ever an employee in the history of the world that should be given generous time off, it has to be a pastor.[26]

---

[26] As an additional thought on this, consider the fact that pastoring is not a 40 hour/week kind of job. In a very real sense, it never ends. There are no days off from loving your people and being concerned about them. There is no vacation from one's responsibility to care for their souls. Again, if there was ever a "job" that should be provided with as much PTO as possible, it has to be the job of a pastor.

Planned Sabbaticals

In addition to PTO, churches should provide a regular schedule of planned sabbaticals for each pastoral staff member. This is slightly different than vacation in that it should be designed to provide each pastor with an opportunity to "recharge his own spiritual batteries" for an extended period of time.

I learned this lesson the hard way. I had served as the lead pastor of our church for a little over seven years before I took my first sabbatical. In retrospect, that was probably two years too long. By the time I had spent seven years pastoring our church, I was empty. In those seven years, we had tripled in size, doubled in staff, purchased a building, and reoriented almost every facet of our ministry philosophy and practice. It had been the most challenging seven years of my life . . . and of our marriage . . . and, to be completely transparent, I was on the verge of quitting.

Thankfully, my dear friends and fellow Elders stepped in and forced me to take a two-month sabbatical. I was completely relieved of every pastoral and administrative duty, and was even excluded from the vast majority of emails about church-related items or issues during that time. They gave me a book or two to read, and asked me to spend extended times in God's Word and in prayer. They even provided me with a budget of $1,500 to get away with my family for relaxation and refreshment. Without any exaggeration, I can honestly say that those two months changed my life.

As I reflect on it now, I believe that every pastor should be given a similar benefit at least once every five years, if not more often.

Retirement

Pastors should be provided with a generous retirement plan by their churches. However, because this issue is so large and so unique, I will address it separately in the next chapter.

What Does All of This Mean for You?

As the employee, you may not feel that you are in a place to ask for the benefits listed above. While I understand that feeling completely, the fact of the matter is that your church may not know that they should be thinking about these things unless you bring it up to them. That was my experience.

As stated earlier, for the first five years I was a pastor, I was provided with health and dental coverage and an undefined amount of PTO. I had no vision or disability coverage, no planned sabbaticals, and no retirement.

Eventually, two things forced me to go to one of our Elders and ask for the remaining items. First, the needs of my family reached a point that I felt I had to ask. We hadn't been to an eye doctor in years. Due to the misunderstanding we had about my initial pastoral income, I had been forced to cash-in our small 401(k) to prevent us from going bankrupt, and we had no retirement. Something had to be done about these things, and if I didn't bring it up, I knew no one would.

Second, the thought of additional or future pastors of our church going through the same things I had experienced motivated me to do something to protect them from a similar situation. At the time I approached that Elder about adding these benefits, we were already having discussions about bringing on a second, full-time, pastoral employee. I remember sitting at my desk thinking about his family, and

I knew that I could not leave things as they were. Something had to be done.

For these same reasons, I encourage you to let your church know that you need these benefits, that your family needs them, and that any future or additional pastors of your church will need them.

As suggested earlier, I think you should buy each Elder, Deacon, Trustee, committee member, or whoever it is that makes decisions about pastoral compensation in your church a copy of my book, *Structuring Pastoral Compensation: A Practical Guide for Blessing Your Pastor*, so that they can begin to understand the many and varied components that go into providing a comprehensive benefits package for pastoral employees.

Remember, they don't know what they don't know. If you need these things, but you don't tell them . . . then that's on you.

Once you tell them, be patient and understanding. They may not be able to do everything all at once. Maybe these things will become goals to aim for over time. My experience has shown me that this is often enough. As long as I know that my church loves me and is thinking about these things for me, I can patiently wait for our circumstances to change.

CHAPTER 6
RETIREMENT

"Go to the ant, O sluggard; consider her ways and be wise."

-Proverbs 6:6-

• • •

I will never forget how sick I felt the day I cashed in our small 401(k). It wasn't much – only about $7,000 – but it was the only retirement savings we had. Imagine how much sicker I felt the day I mailed my Form 4361 to the IRS opting out of Social Security! Now, we had nothing for the future.

As the years passed, that feeling of sickness grew in my heart. Even after our situation improved, I had not been able to set aside anything for retirement, and our church did not have any kind of retirement plan for us at the time. I could feel the effects of time passing me by, and I knew I had to act. I reached out to one of our Elders, pleaded my case, and prayed for God to provide.

Even though the prior chapter was on the topic of benefits, I just felt that this particular benefit was so unique and important that it deserved separate and special treatment.

Let me begin by sorting out two groups of churches right off the bat. If you are the pastor of a church that is a part of a denomination or group that provides either A) automatic retirement contributions for you, and/or B) a guaranteed pension for you, then this chapter may or may not be necessary. I am primarily writing for those pastors who do not have the privilege of one of the two scenarios listed above.

The fact of the matter is that every pastor needs to be planning for retirement AND every church needs to participate in that retirement plan.[27]

For churches that do not have the option of using a denominational retirement and/or pension package, there are three main options for providing a retirement benefit for pastoral employees. I will list them in order of my least favorite to my most favorite.

SIMPLE IRA ACCOUNTS
As the name suggests, SIMPLE IRAs are extremely simple for churches to operate. SIMPLE plans can be set up as either matching or non-matching plans. If a church chooses to use the matching approach, they can match, dollar-for-dollar, each employee's retirement contributions up to 3% of the employee's total salary.[28]

---

[27] I have written a book for pastors to help them understand the world of investing. *The Pastor's Guide to Wise Investing* is available on Amazon and at my website (www.brokepastor.com).

[28] For pastors, please note that this only applies to their actual salary, not their total income. If a pastor has a total income of $50,000, but designates $30,000 of that as being housing allowance, the church can only match his contributions up to $600 ($20,000 x 3% = $600).

They can do less than 3%, but no more. In this setup, employees can also contribute up to $12,500 towards their SIMPLE plan as of 2017.[29]

If the church chooses to use the non-matching approach, they must contribute 2% of every employee's salary towards their respective SIMPLE plans regardless of whether or not the employee makes any contribution.

What I like about SIMPLE plans is that they are simple. They are extremely easy to set up and administrate. What I hate about SIMPLE plans is that the church can only contribute a very small amount towards the pastor's retirement account.

Obviously, a lot more could be said about the intricacies of and requirements surrounding SIMPLE IRAs.[30] I am not an accountant, tax professional, or certified financial planner, and you should definitely seek counsel from one or more of these individuals before deciding on which plan is best for you and your church.

However, while it is definitely better than nothing, my non-credentialed belief is that you can do a lot better than a SIMPLE IRA.

403(B) ACCOUNTS

The non-profit equivalent of a 401(k) account is called a 403(b) account. If you have ever had a 401(k), then you know how it works.

---

[29] Employees 50 and older can make an additional $3,000 in catch-up contributions as of 2017.

[30] For a nice overview of SIMPLE IRAs, visit https://www.irs.gov/retirement-plans/plan-sponsor/simple-ira-plan.

However, unless your church is very large, I can almost guarantee that this will not be the best choice for you.

What I like about 403(b) accounts is that there is a lot more flexibility for increased contributions from both the pastor and the church. What I hate about 403(b) accounts is that they are MUCH more complicated to operate and administer, and I would not recommend creating such a plan without the direct help of both an accountant and a tax professional.

Again, a lot more could be said about the intricacies of and requirements surrounding 403(b)s.[31] Since I am not an accountant, tax professional, or certified financial planner, you should definitely seek counsel from one or more of these individuals before deciding on which plan is best for you and your church – particularly if what's best is a 403(b).

SEP IRA ACCOUNTS

Of the three main options available, my favorite option for churches looking to establish a retirement plan for their pastors is a SEP IRA. The most obvious difference between a SEP and either a SIMPLE or 403(b) is that employees are not allowed to make contributions to a SEP. Only the employer can contribute.

In my experience, this isn't an issue for most pastors since most pastors probably don't have a ton of money to contribute towards retirement out of their own budgets anyway; and even if they do, they can usually

---

[31] For a nice overview of 403(b)s, visit https://www.irs.gov/retirement-plans/irc-403b-tax-sheltered-annuity-plans.

still do so through making contributions to their own personal, traditional or Roth IRA.

The biggest thing I like about the SEP IRA is that the church can choose to contribute up to 25% of the pastor's total salary towards his retirement.[32] This provides both the pastor and the church with a multitude of options regarding how to best care for the pastor and his family.

As for what I don't like about SEPs . . . yeah, I can't think of anything. They're easy to set up and operate. They provide a way for the church to be as generous as it can afford to be to all employees. There really is no downside that I can see.

Obviously, a lot more could be said about the intricacies of and requirements surrounding SEPs.[33] In case it isn't clear by this point, I am not an accountant, tax professional, or certified financial planner, and you should definitely seek counsel from one or more of these individuals before deciding on which plan is best for you and your church.

What Does All of This Mean for You?
Like I said in the previous chapter, it means you need to talk with your Elders, Deacons, Trustees, committee members, or whoever it is that

---

[32] As with SIMPLE plans, please note that this only applies to the pastor's actual salary, not their total income. If a pastor has a total income of $50,000, but designates $30,000 of that as being housing allowance, the church can only contribute up to $5,000 ($20,000 x 25% = $5,000).

[33] For a nice overview of SEP IRAs, visit https://www.irs.gov/retirement-plans/plan-sponsor/simplified-employee-pension-plan-sep.

makes decisions about pastoral compensation in your church. They need to think through these various options and get counsel from the appropriate professionals so that they can make the best possible decision regarding how to best provide for your retirement.

Anything is better than nothing. So, if you don't currently have a church-sponsored retirement plan of any sort, recognize that any of the three options above will be a huge improvement.[34]

---

[34] In Chapter 6 of my companion guide, *Structuring Pastoral Compensation: A Practical Guide for Blessing Your Pastor*, I work through this same information from the perspective of church decision makers and include a few more practical suggestions.

Chapter 7
Accountable Reimbursement Plans

"Be wise as serpents and innocent as doves."

-Matthew 10:16-

• • •

In my personal opinion, one of the absolute best things that a church can provide for its pastor is a clear and generous accountable reimbursement plan.[35]

An accountable reimbursement plan is, in effect, an agreement by the church to reimburse the pastor for certain, defined expenses assuming said expenses can be properly documented.

Or, to put it in plain English, the church will pay you back for an agreed-upon expense if you can prove it with a receipt. That's the simplest way to understand it.

---

[35] For complete IRS rules, see: https://www.irs.gov/publications/p463/ch06.html#en_US_2016_publink100034114.

Non-Accountable Plans

Now, before continuing, let me just point out the word "accountable." This is here because, in the world of reimbursements, there are two types of plans that employers can use: A) accountable plans, and B) non-accountable plans.

If in an accountable plan, an employee has to prove an expense with a receipt before it can be reimbursed, then you may rightly assume that, in a non-accountable plan, no proof is needed.

For example, let's say that Pastor Bob receives $300/month from his church to cover wear and tear on his personal vehicle related to his pastoral duties. Pastor Bob never has to justify that amount by turning in any mileage logs or receipts. He just gets that same amount every month no matter how much or how little he drives. This is a non-accountable reimbursement plan.

While that may seem like a great benefit at first, let me assure you that it is a headache waiting to happen! On the one hand, let's say Pastor Bob's actual vehicle expenses for the year total $3,800. Remember, he only received $3,600. Who pays the difference? He does! He can't go back and ask for the difference since that is not how the plan was set up. Whatever he gets is what he gets . . . which means that he is effectively taking a $200 pay cut at that point by having to pay the difference between the non-accountable reimbursement and his actual work-related expenses out of his own pocket.

On the other hand, let's say his actual vehicle expenses for the year are only $3,000. Does he get to keep the $600 difference as tax-free income? No! He can either return the unused portion to the church OR he can report the surplus $600 he received as being taxable income. He has to do one or the other.

This is why I said that non-accountable plans are just headaches waiting to happen. Either the pastor will end up having to cover a certain amount of expenses out of his own pocket or he will have to give back OR claim as taxable income any surplus. There is a much easier and more equitable way of doing this.

Accountable Plans

As already stated, in an accountable reimbursement plan, a pastor can be reimbursed for certain defined expenses as long as those expenses can be proven to be valid. Let's break this down into a few components.

You Have to Have a Plan

Yes, I mean a real one. Something written down. A policy. Accountable plans should not be enacted or administered willy-nilly. You should put in writing the exact details of whatever arrangement you come up with.

Now, saying that it has to be written doesn't mean that it has to be complicated. In fact, these can be very concise and simple. At the bare minimum, your plan should clearly list what types of expenses are considered reimbursable, what amounts or percentages of said expenses will be reimbursed, who is eligible for these reimbursements, and any other pertinent details you feel need to be included.[36]

Work-Related Expenses

As for what can be reimbursed, there is no single, authoritative list that I can give you. The general rule-of-thumb is that only genuine, work-

---

[36] I offer policy templates, including an Accountable Reimbursement Plan template, on my website (www.brokepastor.com).

related expenses can be reimbursed. This would be specific to each employee's job responsibilities.

For example, while Pastor Bob (acting in his official capacity as a pastor) may be reimbursed for buying a cup of coffee while meeting a church member at a local coffee shop to discuss a counseling issue, Janitor John would likely not be eligible for getting that same reimbursement since his job responsibilities most likely do not include counseling. Does that make sense?[37]

Types of Reimbursements
As long as the reimbursed expense can be reasonably justified as being within the bounds of the employee's job responsibilities, pretty much anything could be considered a reimbursable expense. That said, a few are considered fairly common.

Mileage
Like many other employees, pastors are often required to drive their own personal vehicles in the fulfillment of their work responsibilities. And so, like those other employees, they are entitled to be reimbursed at the standard IRS rate.[38]

---

[37] While it may not need to be stated, I'll do it just to be safe – a family member of a pastor is, generally, not eligible for reimbursements unless they are also employees of the church (e.g. a pastor's wife who meets a lady from the church at a local coffee shop to discuss a counseling issue is normally not eligible to receive a reimbursement for her expenses unless she is also an employee).

[38] Generally speaking, it's probably safest to assume that a pastor cannot be reimbursed for driving to and from his primary place of business.

The process here is simple. The pastor should simply record any mileage incurred due to work-related travel and should report that mileage to the church on a regular basis (e.g. weekly, monthly, etc.).

Travel and Entertainment

One of the most common reimbursable expenses pastors incur is that of travel and entertainment. This is not the same as a mileage reimbursement. This has to do with expenses incurred either on a trip (e.g. to a conference, missions trip, etc.) or in relation to meals (whether attached to a trip or not).

For example, if your church sends you (in your official capacity as a pastor) on a trip to a national conference, then you can be reimbursed all reasonable expenses associated with your travel (i.e. airfare, hotel, meals, etc.).

Or, more commonly, if you meet someone (again, in your official capacity as a pastor) for lunch or coffee, you can usually be reimbursed for all reasonable expenses associated therewith.

Continuing Professional Education/Improvement

A church can designate a certain amount of funds to be available to a pastor for continuing professional, ministerial education or improvement. This could include the cost of books, classes, conferences, subscriptions, professional dues, or other related expenses.

Cell Phone/Internet

If the church expects its pastor to use his own cell phone or home internet to complete church-related work responsibilities, then the church should reimburse the pastor for some portion of those expenses.

In my case, I work from home. When we built our church's building in 2012, we purposefully chose to not include any office space for employees. As such, the church reimburses me for the cost of maintaining a cell phone and for the cost of providing an internet connection.[39]

On a related note, it is my understanding that home phone expenses cannot be reimbursed, generally speaking.

Home Office

Similar to cell/internet reimbursements, home office expenses may be reimbursable . . . assuming that the pastor is required to use a home office. This could cover things like computers, printers, toner, paper, etc.

If the pastor is provided with an office within the church building, home office expenses will likely not be reimbursable.

Clothing/Uniform

If your church requires you to wear a certain type of clothing or uniform in the performance of your pastoral duties, such clothing/uniform expenses may be reimbursable.

---

[39] It is important to note that only *my* expenses are reimbursed. My family's total cell phone and internet bill exceeds the reimbursable amount provided by the church. I am responsible for the remainder.

Reimbursement Amounts
By and large, the expenses listed above should be reimbursed in full. However, churches may elect to only reimburse a percentage of these expenses for various reasons. If you are not fully reimbursed for legitimate work-related expenses, you may be able to claim the unreimbursed amount as a deduction on your taxes.

Required Documentation
To be an accountable plan, you must give an account for your reimbursement requests. The most common way to document an expense is with a receipt. In theory, you may also be able to use bank/credit card statements, invoices, or anything else that proves you incurred a reimbursable expense.

Reporting/Retention Tools
Reimbursable expenses can be reported in physical form (i.e. turning in physical receipts), or in electronic form (i.e. utilizing a service such as Expensify®).[40] If you require receipts to be physically submitted, it is best to retain those for at least three years. If you use an online service such as Expensify®, they will do all of the document retention for you.

WHY I LOVE REIMBURSABLE PLANS

I love reimbursable plans because they are, in effect, tax-free pay raises.[41] If I wasn't being reimbursed for these expenses, I would still have to pay for them out of my own pocket! But by reimbursing me

---

[40] We have just recently begun using Expensify®, and we will NEVER go back to physical receipts! Expensify® is not a sponsor of this book.

[41] Practically, not technically.

for these expenses, I am allowed to keep more of my actual salary to be used for truly personal expenses.

What Does All of This Mean for You?
Again, like I said in the previous chapter, it means you need to talk with your Elders, Deacons, Trustees, committee members, or whoever it is that makes decisions about the annual budget for your church.

In our budget, we have a section designated exclusively to accountable reimbursements. We also have policies built around the various items that we have approved for reimbursement.

If your church does not have these things, and if you do not know how to talk with your church about it, then may I again suggest that you purchase a copy of the companion guide to this book, *Structuring Pastoral Compensation*, for every decision maker within your church so that they can begin to learn about the benefits of providing you with an accountable reimbursement plan.

Chapter 8
Putting the Pieces Together

"Commit your work to the Lord, and your plans will be established."

-Proverbs 16:3-

• • •

Well, I feel like I should begin by apologizing for sounding like a broken record up to this point. Over and over again, I have asked you to wait until Chapter 8 to see how all of the things we've talked about above can be used to work together for your benefit.

However, I still believe that this has been the best approach. Before you could think through a comprehensive plan, you needed to understand all of the basic components. The previous chapters have given you a primer on those components. But now, after much waiting, it's time to put the pieces together.

Making a Decision about Social Security
If you are still within the window of making a decision about whether or not to opt out of Social Security, let me encourage you to not delay in arriving at a decision. As far as I am concerned, there is no right or

wrong answer to this question. As long as you are honest with yourself about your motivations, you can feel confident that you have done the right thing.

While financial considerations cannot be your primary motivation, I feel that I should take a moment to point out the pros and cons of either decision from a financial perspective.

If you choose to opt out, you may gain extra money in your monthly paycheck now, but you may lose the opportunity of getting much or any financial, medical, or disability help from Social Security when you retire. That puts ALL of the risk for your financial future squarely on your own shoulders.

If you choose to stay in, you may lose 15.3% of your total income to SECA each year, but you will have the comfort of knowing that Social Security and Medicare will likely be a part of your overall retirement picture.

Which is better? I don't know, nor does it matter. Your decision must be made apart from these things, but I do want you to know what you are choosing regardless of which choice you make.

Choose wisely.

Balancing Salary and Housing Allowance

I believe that the single most important component of managing your pastoral compensation wisely is determining the right balance between your salary and your housing allowance.

Keeping Taxes in Mind
How much "taxable income" is right for you? While you may, at first, be tempted to think that the answer is $0, I can almost assure you that this is not the case.

Because a pastor's housing allowance isn't counted as taxable income, the only portion of your total income that the IRS uses to calculate not only your taxes, but also your refundable and non-refundable tax credits, is your actual salary.

On the one hand, in terms of taxes, you may want to increase your housing allowance (within the ethical and reasonable bounds described in Chapter 4) so that you do not have to pay any income tax on your earnings . . . or at least as little as possible. This is even more true if you have a second job or if your spouse is employed.

On the other hand, have you ever heard of something called the Earned Income Credit (EIC)? For most lower income taxpayers with dependents (which likely includes the vast majority of pastors), this is the single largest portion of their annual tax refund. If you don't know how the EIC works, it is based off of an easy-to-read table that works something like a bell curve.[42]

For example, in 2016, the highest EIC credit available to a married couple, filing jointly, with two dependents was $5,572. However, this amount was only available to taxpayers whose adjusted gross income (for EIC purposes) on their 1040 fell between $13,900 and $23,750. If

---

[42] For the 2016 tax year, see: https://apps.irs.gov/app/vita/content/globalmedia/earned_income_credit_table_1040i.pdf

you were either above or below that number, then your EIC was reduced.

Common sense, then, would suggest that you would not want to reduce your salary any lower than you had to since it could reduce the amount of EIC (and other tax credits) you may receive at tax time.[43]

Obviously, each pastor's tax situation is different, and I cannot provide you with specific advice on how to think through your own tax ramifications. Just be aware that you want to find the sweet spot between too much and too little taxable income so as to maximize your tax refund.

Keeping Your Home in Mind
At the same time, it only makes sense to maximize your housing allowance as much as you reasonably can. As I will argue in Chapter 9, in the current tax environment that we find ourselves in, the United States government is effectively encouraging and enabling pastors to invest in their own homes like no one else.

This could be done through making improvements or repairs to your home that can be classified as valid housing-related expenses. Or, better yet, this could be done by making extra principal payments on

---

[43] While we can debate whether it is fair or not, in the current tax system in which we all operate, most married pastors (with children) that I know tend to receive very large tax returns each year. It's not because they are doing anything unethical or illegal. It is merely an outworking of the way our income is treated by the IRS. This could change at any time, so I would suggest viewing it as a blessing for as long as it lasts.

your mortgage so as to pay your home off sooner. Either way, you will likely benefit directly.

Keeping Obamacare in Mind
If your church provides you with health insurance paid for by the church or the denomination to which you belong, then this will not apply to you.

But for those of us who have opted to get our insurance through one of the Obamacare exchanges, our premium and cost savings subsidies are directly based on our modified adjusted gross income (MAGI).

That means that setting our housing allowance too high or too low could have a drastic effect on how much we pay for health coverage. However, unlike pretty much every other employee in the world, pastors have the ability to control, via their housing allowance designation, how much MAGI they end up reporting at tax time.[44]

Keeping Retirement in Mind
As noted in Chapter 6, retirement contributions made by your church into a SEP are based on your actual salary, not your total income. Let's say Pastor Bob makes $50,000/year but designates $25,000 as being his housing allowance. If his church contributes 5% of his salary into his SEP, he will receive $1,250 in retirement contributions. However, if he designates $30,000 as being his housing allowance, he will only receive $1,000. If he designates $20,000, he will receive $1,500.

---

[44] See my other book, *Benefitting from Obamacare*, for how our church handled this.

Finding the Right Balance

So, in order to find the right balance between salary and housing allowance, you will need to take whichever of these four issues that apply to you into account. Again, I wish I could help do that for you, but since each pastor's situation is so different, there is no one-size-fits-all approach.

What I can do, though, is share how my own balance has shifted over the years so that you can get an idea of how these things work together.

For example, in the early days of being a pastor, I was not provided with a retirement plan by our church. However, we were provided with medical insurance coverage since Obamacare was not an option yet. At that time, I designated about two-thirds of my income as being housing allowance (approximately $30,000). Since my only issue to consider at that point was maximizing my tax benefit, this placed me in a great position to get my maximum possible tax refund.

Today, a number of things have changed. Ten years into ministry, I now make more money than I did when I started. While our house has gone up in value, I continue to keep my fair-market rental valuation well within the ethical and realistic range. I now have a SEP, and I also now get my health insurance through one of the Obamacare exchanges.

Practically, what that means is that I now split my income approximately 50/50 between salary and housing allowance. This keeps my salary low enough that I am able to get (almost) the maximum subsidy on my health insurance while, at the same time, still qualifying for some EIC credit, AND maximizing my salary so that I can get the largest possible SEP contribution from our church while, at the same time, providing me with the opportunity to pay ahead on the principal of our home mortgage, thus saving me money on mortgage interest. In other words, I'm benefitting on all four fronts!

This kind of balancing isn't necessarily easy, but neither is it hard. Every year, I just have to recheck all my numbers against whatever changes have occurred since the prior year. I check the EIC tables, I check the Obamacare exchange income limits, I confirm with our church what they are willing to contribute towards our SEP, and I try to determine what, if any, repairs or improvements need to be made to our home.

In addition, I am always cognizant of our current situation in life. Do the kids need braces this year? How far away am I from having to pay for college? What condition are our cars in? You know . . . the normal things of life.

Once I've taken all of that into account, I arrive at a number that makes the most sense based on all of the issues above. It's probably 60% art and 40% science, and over the years, I have made mistakes.

But the more I've done this, the more I've learned which components matter the most for our family, and the better I have gotten at striking the right balance. I know the same will be true for you.

Balancing Cash Compensation Against Other Options

The longer I have served as a pastor, the more I have come to appreciate forms of compensation that aren't, technically, considered income or cash compensation.

I'm referring specifically to increased benefits, increased retirement contributions, and increased reimbursable expenses.

Because my current situation is so complex (particularly related to Obamacare), the balancing act I do between my salary and my housing allowance is very delicate. The truth of the matter is – I don't want to make any more money than I do today! At least, not in terms of income.

So, because our church loves us and wants to continue improving our compensation package year-over-year, what else can they do? Well, they can increase the three things I just mentioned.

As it stands today, our church pays the full premiums for the various forms of insurance still provided for us (since medical insurance is no longer needed or desired). By not having us pay any portion of those premiums, they effectively put more money in our pockets without raising our income one cent.

This is also one of the reasons why I love SEP IRAs. The church can contribute up to 25% of my total salary (not housing allowance) to our SEP. That's a large percentage, and it gives the church a lot of wiggle room to grow over time in providing for our retirement. Think of the blessing they will be to us if they just go up 1% every year! The more they contribute for us, the less obligated I feel to do so out of our own pocket, thus providing us with a *de facto*, tax-free raise each time they increase their contribution.[45]

---

[45] That doesn't mean that we shouldn't be contributing to our own retirement. In fact, my wife works two days a week just so we can save additional money for retirement. Planning for retirement is, ultimately, our responsibility, but to the extent our church helps us with that, it certainly removes a great deal of stress related to the issue.

Adding reimbursements is the third way they can put more money into our pockets without increasing our income. This year is the first year we have had a mileage reimbursement plan. My guess is that, by the end of the year, we will be reimbursed about $1,000 towards work-related mileage. Well, I would have incurred those expenses whether or not our church reimbursed us for them (I mean, I've done so for the nine previous years), but this year, I'll actually get reimbursed for them! I view that as a $1,000, tax-free, pay raise.

WHAT DOES ALL OF THIS MEAN FOR YOU?
It means that you need to be wise as a serpent and innocent as a dove when it comes to your pastoral finances. If what I've written up to this point sounds cold and calculating, it's because it is . . . in a way. That's just a normal component of handling money. You have to be wise as a serpent – being a good steward of what God, your church, and the government have put in front of you. You have to take full advantage of every benefit that could be yours.

At the same time, I want you to be as innocent as a dove. I don't, in any way, want you to do anything unethical (obviously), nor do I want you to do anything that will go against your conscience.[46] That said, sometimes our consciences need to be informed and shown that they are being too sensitive. If that describes you, you will have to wrestle with this issue before God.

A good friend of mine once reminded me of an old saying: "it's a sin to evade taxes, not to avoid them." In other words, if we are doing things to evade paying for what we are supposed to pay for, that is a

---

[46] Romans 14:23.

sin. But if we take advantage of what is ethically and legally presented to us to avoid paying for things we don't need to, that is called wisdom.

And so, I encourage you to consider what I have written very carefully; talk about these things with your Elders or Deacons or Trustees; and pray that God will give you wisdom and patience to do what is right.

SECTION 2

Chapter 9
The Pastor's House

"For every house is built by someone, but the builder of all things is God."

-Hebrews 3:4-

• • •

Our first (and still our current) home was a mistake. I say that somewhat tongue-in-cheek because, in God's good grace, he turned what was definitely a lemon into lemonade. But apart from God's grace, our home was a mistake. We should have never, ever purchased it . . . or even have been able to purchase it.

It was August of 2007, the end of the housing bubble, and my wife and I had to move from the Chicagoland area to Virginia Beach in about three weeks. Based on my impending "tax-free" pastoral salary of $48,000/year, the bank approved us for a loan of up to $260,000!

Now, you might read that and think that we were rolling in money. Surely, $260,000 could buy most people a small mansion! But not in Virginia Beach, and not in 2007.

After spending two straight days looking at homes during a whirlwind, weekend visit, I selected a 1451 square foot, three bedroom, two bath ranch sitting on about a fifth of an acre of land that was a "fixer upper" to say the least. Truth be told, it was a complete and total mess. It needed new windows, new HVAC, new flooring, a new roof, and a complete interior and exterior cosmetic facelift. And here's the kicker – it was the cheapest house in our neighborhood!

Sure, there were cheaper homes in other neighborhoods, but if I knew anything as a twenty-nine-year-old, first-time homebuyer, I knew that the three words that mattered most in real estate were, "location, Location, LOCATION!" And out of all the homes I had visited over those two days, no other house even came close to the location of the one we would eventually buy.

The problem was (as if all the problems listed above weren't enough) it was at the very top of our price range. Sure, we could afford it (especially on $48,000/year "tax-free"). We would just have to trim back some other areas: maybe not set aside money for savings, maybe go without food on Tuesdays . . .

Whatever it took, I was sure we could find a way. So, undeterred, I pressed on!

Do you have any moments in life where, if you could go back in time and slap yourself, you would? This is one of mine.

Had we known about the effects of SECA, we would have never bought our house. Had SECA never happened, maybe we would have been okay . . . a little thinner . . . but okay.

However, as you already know, neither of those things happened, and we bought a house that we could not afford at the very beginning of my transition to the pastorate. Talk about stress! Talk about a rude awakening!

As I sit here, in that same house, ten years later, typing these words, I am thankful to say that I can do so with a smile and with a lot more wisdom than I had ten years prior.

And if I did have a time machine that would enable me to go back and talk to my twenty-nine-year-old self, rather than slapping him, I think I would give him the following advice.

Your Greatest Financial Investment

It's often said that a home is the average person's single greatest investment. While this is likely true for the average person, I can now say that it is doubly true for a pastor.

Because of the amazing benefit of your housing allowance, the United States government is effectively enabling and encouraging you to buy and pay off IN FULL a home . . . and then maybe another . . . and then maybe another still.

If I could do things over again, I would have purchased the cheapest home that I could find that A) needed little or no repair, and B) that I believed I could either rent or sell with little difficulty in the future.

The reason for this comes back to the pastor's housing allowance. Remember, a pastor can designate a portion of his salary as being housing allowance, thus shielding it from income taxes. In Chapter 4, I suggested that you determine the fair-market rental value of your home, fully furnished, with utilities, before designating your housing allowance.

Like with our home, your home will have a reasonable spectrum of value that is neither unjustifiably high nor low. Obviously, the amount you decide on within that spectrum will depend on all of the factors discussed in Chapter 8, but from my own personal experience, I would highly recommend that you choose (or work towards choosing over time as your financial situation improves) the higher end of that spectrum.

The reason for this suggestion is so that you can set aside as much cash as possible for paying off your home early since payments on your mortgage, whether required or voluntary, generally count as valid housing expenses.

Both Dave Ramsey and Crown Financial Ministries have done an excellent job of emphasizing the importance of this to Christian audiences across the country and around the world for many years now. And while it is certainly true for believers (and non-believers as well), I think that pastors may be in the best place of anyone to actually do this.

Imagine if my wife and I had purchased a condo or townhome that was in good shape and was half of what we paid for our current home. Over time, as we could reasonably increase our housing allowance, we would have had more and more cash to put towards the prepayment of our mortgage.

I'm not saying we would have paid it off in five or ten years from the date of purchase, but I don't think paying it off in fifteen would have been out of the question. If we had done that, we would be five years away from owning our home outright!

However, this idea doesn't stop there. When a lay person pays off their mortgage, they can continue to live in their home and use the freed-up cash towards other things.

Pastors are different. If I were to pay off my home today, I would not be able to come up with enough expenses to justify my current housing allowance . . . which means that of the three numbers that the IRS looks at (amount designated, actual expenses, and fair-market rental value), my housing allowance would automatically be reduced to the actual expense category. This means I would have more taxable income which would throw off all of the other factors I need to balance. What should I do?

Well, to put it directly, I should buy another house! The IRS only allows pastors to claim expenses/housing allowance for the home they actually live in. That means I couldn't simply stay in my current home and buy another to rent out. It means that I would have to leave my home and purchase a second home in order to bring my housing expenses back in line with my designation/fair-market rental value.

If I wanted, I could sell my current home, and use the proceeds to buy a more expensive home. This would allow me to make a large down payment, but still keep a mortgage that I could use to maximize my annual housing allowance through making extra principal payments.

Or, if I wanted, I could keep my current home, but move out of it and buy a second home. This would then allow me to rent out my first home for additional income while I began the process of paying off the second home through making additional principal payments out of my housing allowance.

What I Wish I Had Done

Basically, what I'm saying to you is that as long as you are a pastor, you need to have a mortgage that you are using as a tool to maximize the value of your housing allowance. Whether that is through "buying up" over time for your own personal residence, or through building a portfolio of rental properties that will provide income for you into the future – one way or the other, you cannot and should not allow this amazing benefit provided only to ministers pass you by.

For me, I wish I had gone with the rental approach. I wish we had bought a cheaper home, paid it off, moved out, bought a second house, and then rented the first.

I would have taken the income from the rent and added it to my extra principal payments on our second home in order to pay that one off even faster. I would then repeat the process again and again and again for as long as I could.

So, if you already own a home, see if you can pay it off by diverting as much of your housing allowance as possible towards making prepayments on your mortgage. When you pay it off, buy another house and pay that off!

If you haven't bought a house yet, or are just getting started in ministry, consider the thoughts above. I wish I had known these things when I was getting started.

Chapter 10
Pay Yourself Second

"For where your treasure is, there your heart will be also."

-Matthew 6:21-

• • •

Have you ever heard the saying, "Pay yourself first"? The more reading I do in the realm of personal finance, the more I see it. However, as Christians, I think we need to tweak the saying just a bit.

A Biblical Adjustment
When it comes to the arena of general, personal finance, the slogan "Pay Yourself First" is a helpful guide for thinking about what to do with your money.

As a believer, I would just move it one step over to second place as I believe, wholeheartedly, that the first "payment" we make out of our income should be to the Lord.

I hate to say it, but I've known pastors who don't give. That's not an exaggeration for the sake of illustration. That's the honest truth. And while there may be reasons for that, I just think that pastors need to model, to whatever extent they can in their given circumstances, what it looks like to be generous with the income God gives them. They need to learn to "pay" God first.

However, this isn't a book about giving, and now that I have that out of the way, you should now understand the reason I titled this chapter what I did.

I believe that the Christian version of "Pay Yourself First" is "Pay Yourself Second." What this means is that, after you give to God, the very next thing you should do with your money is to use it to prepare for your own financial future.

A Three-Fold Approach

In his book, *Rich Dad Poor Dad*, Robert Kiyosaki does an excellent job of showing how the rich make it their mission in life to use their income to build wealth before ever paying out any expenses.

In other words, when money comes into your bank account, the first thing you should do with it after giving to the Lord is to provide for yourself financially. For the average pastor, this will likely mean three things.

First, it will mean building an adequate emergency savings fund. This money will come out of the salary portion of your income. Every month, before you pay any bills, you should set aside money to cover emergency expenses. A good rule-of-thumb is that you should have between three and six months' worth of living expenses in your emergency savings. It may take you a while to get there, but if you keep saving, you will arrive at that goal before you know it.

Second, you should open and begin funding either a traditional or Roth IRA out of the salary portion of your income. Again, this doesn't have to be a super-large amount each month. It just needs to be something.

By the way, this is regardless of whether or not your church provides you with a retirement plan. No matter what, you need to be saving for a time when you will no longer be able to work, and IRAs are probably one of the best ways to do this for most pastors.[47]

Third, out of your housing allowance, you should make an extra principal payment on your mortgage. You say, "But I need to use my housing allowance for repairs on my home." Ok. I get that because I had to do the same. Sometimes, the most I could pay ahead on our mortgage in a given month was $25, but I tried to pay something . . . and you should too.

A Longer-Term Focus

Once you have built an adequate emergency savings, you should continue to pay yourself second by diverting whatever money you were putting into savings towards your retirement.

Along the way, as your income increases, you should make it a requirement that a certain portion of each pay increase is automatically set apart towards these goals.

For far too many people - pastors included – an increase in salary automatically means an increase in expenses (i.e. they begin spending

---

[47] I have written a small booklet titled *The Pastor's Guide to Wise Investing* to help give you guidance on how to think about and begin/continue investing. You can find it at www.brokepastor.com.

whatever extra they get). My plea to you is that you not be like everyone else in this area.

If you receive an extra $1,000/year in salary, give to the Lord out of your increase as you are able, and then commit some amount towards these goals. If you do this each time you receive additional income, you'll never even feel it in your monthly budget, but you will begin to see the benefits of this approach in your long-term planning.

Pay yourself second!

Chapter 11
Considering Your future

"So, whether you eat or drink, or whatever you do, do all to the glory of God."

-1 Corinthians 10:31-

• • •

It seems to me that there are two kinds of pastors: A) those who can't ever imagine doing or being anything else, and B) those who can. It just so happens that I fall into the second category.

I have served as the lead pastor of our church for over ten years. I have no doubt or question that God brought our family here and that I was supposed to pastor our church. I love our church; our whole family does.

But even as I say all of those things, the fact of the matter is that I am totally open to anything else God might have for me outside of pastoring . . . and I do mean anything. As it stands today, I may be a pastor for the rest of my life or I may not. I'm trying to hold that question loosely since I have no idea what God has in store for us.

And as I've thought about that over the years, I have recognized how important it is for pastors to use their time and resources wisely to prepare themselves for whatever God may have for them next – regardless of which kind of pastor they would define themselves as being. Because, quite frankly, none of us know what God may have for us to do in the future.

So, to that end, here are two suggestions.

Expand Your Horizons

Whether you want to spend the rest of your life as a pastor or not, you should expand your horizons beyond the world of ministry through reading, learning, and doing.

First, you should begin reading books outside the world of theology and ministry. What interests you? For me, I have an intense natural interest in the world of business, personal finance, productivity, and leadership. Some of the best books I've read over the past ten years have come from those subject fields and have been used by God to not only improve my ministry, but also to broaden my thoughts about other opportunities that are out there.

Second, you should become a student of non-ministry related topics. Go to a seminar on real estate. Take a class on accounting. Learn to paint or dance . . . or paint while you dance! Just continue to expand your training beyond that of pastoral ministry.

Third, do different things. Start a hobby that requires you to do something. For me, that's kind of the genesis of this book. I've always wanted to write, but had never sat down to just do it. So, I started writing . . . and now, you're reading a book I wrote. How unbelievable is that?!?

Whether you choose to do only one of these three things or all of them, I encourage you to begin to actively expand your horizons beyond that of pastoral ministry so as to make yourself a more well-rounded individual and to see what, if anything, God may do with those things in the future.

Consider Non-Pastoral Opportunities

One of the easiest ways to stretch yourself is to consider taking on some kind of extra "job." Now, as I write this, I know that there are many pastors who simply could not do this if they wanted to. When I was a solo pastor, there would have been no way I could have handled adding anything else to my plate.

However, today, my situation is different. For example, a few years ago, I was asked to serve as an Advisory Council member for the Board of Directors of the seminary from which I graduated. For five years, I was allowed to participate in and observe the inner workings of the seminary. While I may not have contributed very much, I sure learned a ton about Board-level governance and administration. Those are very marketable skills!

As another example, about a year ago, an opportunity presented itself for me to take on a part-time job reviewing residential real estate contracts for a local builder . . . from home! It's not much (I probably average about five hours of work for every two-week pay period), but it has stretched me and taught me new things.

In Robert Kiyosaki's book, *Rich Dad Poor Dad*, he devotes an entire chapter to the idea of working to learn, not to earn. I can now see the wisdom of that advice first-hand.

I seriously doubt that I will ever become either a Realtor® or a residential home builder, but I have learned so much just by watching how the two sides negotiate home prices and concessions and every other little detail of the deal. If I ever end up owning a rental property someday, this job will have prepared me for the business and legal components of those kinds of transactions.

Is there something you could take on, part-time, paid or unpaid, that would give you an opportunity to learn a new skill? It's not about earning extra money.[48] It's about learning skills that will both stretch you and prepare you for whatever God has for you next. If you keep your eyes and ears open, you may be surprised at the opportunities that come along.

---

[48] Though, if you do, see Chapter 10 for how to handle it.

Chapter 12
Seeking Professional Help

"Listen to advice and accept instruction, that you may gain wisdom in the future."

-Proverbs 19:20-

• • •

As I stated at the beginning, I am not a lawyer. Neither am I an accountant, a tax professional, nor a financial planner. I'm just an average pastor of an average church who has spent ten years trying to understand the best way to be "wise as a serpent and innocent as a dove" when it comes to my pastoral compensation.

While I have spent countless hours researching, thinking about, and talking with other pastors and church leaders about these things, I do not want you to base any of your decisions on just my word alone.

Over the years, I have learned the benefit of surrounding myself with great professionals who have helped me sort through the unique intricacies of pastoral compensation issues. You should make it a goal to surround yourself with these same kinds of individuals.

Four Professionals Every Church Should Know

I believe that every church, and by extension, every pastor, should establish a relationship with an attorney, an accountant, a tax professional, and a financial planner.

Now, as I say this, I do not necessarily mean that every church needs to hire these four types of individuals. It just means that you need them. In our church, we have had various relationships with all four of these professions on either a paid or volunteer basis over the years.

Perhaps you have individuals within your church who work in these fields. Have you ever considered asking them for help? I have found that most people within the church, if asked, are more than willing to lend their own professional help whenever they can. If you have them in your church, you should ask them. What's the worst that can happen . . . they might say "No"?

But if you don't have these individuals in your church, you will need to hire them, as needed, either for consultation or for services rendered. Do not look at this as being an expense, but as an investment in the church! I can say that we have never once paid a single dollar to our attorney or our accountant that wasn't worth ten more in money or trouble saved. They have helped us immeasurably over the years, and we are thankful for the relationships we've established.

So, if you don't have these four professionals in your church, get some recommendations from other churches in your area (or, better yet, from business people you respect), and set up some meetings. One way or the other, you will eventually NEED their counsel and help.

Don't Be the "Normal" Church

That said, I'm ashamed to report that what I have heard from some of these professionals over the years is that churches are often their worst clients.

As an example, our CPA has told us repeatedly that, in his 30-plus year career as an accountant, we are the FIRST church with which he has actually been able to have a good and lasting relationship. How sad!

You see, churches are naturally wary of taking on additional expenses, particularly when they don't view the need as being immediate or pressing; and, in addition, many churches seem to think that they should be given these kinds of professional services for free (or really cheap) just because they are a church.

If that is your mindset, please reconsider and repent of these false and selfish beliefs.

There is no CPA, attorney, tax professional, or financial planner that owes you or your church anything. Jesus didn't command them to give you any special treatment just because you're the pastor of a church in town. If you're going to begin working with one of these professionals, be prepared to pay a fair price for their services just like everybody else. Who knows? Maybe they will give you a discount, but don't you dare ask!

Make sure that both you and your church maintain a good reputation with outsiders, and make sure that you establish relationships with these four types of professionals. I promise you . . . doing so will pay dividends later on.

Chapter 13
Final Thoughts

Have you ever wondered if your life was destined to become a cautionary tale?

Of course not. Who would ever think such a thing?

Unfortunately, I must admit that, through the darkness of our financial struggles in the early years of being a pastor, I started to wonder if that's what God was doing in our lives.

And yet, through it all, God used those things to drive one particular passage of Scripture home to me in a way that will forever affect my thinking. It was Jesus' words in Matthew 7:7-11:

> 7 *"Ask, and it will be given to you; seek, and you will find; knock, and it will be opened to you. 8 For everyone who asks receives, and the one who seeks finds, and to the one who knocks it will be opened. 9 Or which one of you, if his son asks him for bread, will give him a stone? 10 Or if he asks for a fish, will give him a serpent? 11 If you then, who are evil, know how to give good gifts to your children, how much more will your Father who is in heaven give good things to those who ask him!*

Now, you might be thinking that the part that stood out was the "Ask, and it will be given to you," part. No. That wasn't it at all. Sure, I asked for all kinds of things during that time, but for most of those requests, the answer was apparently "NO."

What stood out to me was the idea that our Father, being so much better and more loving than us in every imaginable way, will never give his children anything but "bread." Never once will he give us a "stone."

Never.

Sometimes, from my limited and self-centered perspective, I thought he gave me a stone. I mean, to me, it looked like a stone and felt like a stone and tasted like a stone . . . so, obviously . . . it had to be a stone, right?

Wrong.

God has never yet given me, or any of his other children, a stone. He always gives us bread. We may lack the faith and wisdom to see it and appreciate it in the moment, but that doesn't change his promise or his goodness.

Whatever I've gone through, whatever "mistakes" he's allowed me to make, and whatever trials have come our way, God has never failed in his promise to give us bread. Not even once.

I don't know why you've chosen to read this book.

Maybe you find yourself in a tough financial situation because you, like me, didn't know anything about how pastoral finances worked. Or maybe you've been a pastor for a while, but you've been unaware of how to put all the pieces together, and it's had a truly negative effect, both on your soul and your wallet.

I hope these feeble words of mine have helped give you both an understanding of pastoral compensation as well as some ideas for how to move forward. If I can help other pastors avoid going through some of the trials I have gone through (mostly caused by my own ignorance), then writing this book will have been worth it.

To that end, I'd like to humbly ask you to do four things.

First, will you take a few minutes to complete the Next Steps checklist in Appendix B? Doing so will give you a snapshot of where you are today in your pastoral compensation, and will also give you a head start towards implementing some of the ideas from this book.

Second, will you tell other pastors and/or potential pastors about this book? If I could, I would suggest to every Christian college and seminary in America that this should become required reading for anyone and everyone training for pastoral ministry. Would you consider forwarding a link or recommendation to anyone who you think would benefit from this book? I need your help in spreading the word.

Third, will you please share the things I've talked about here with the people in your church who make decisions about pastoral compensation? At the risk of saying it one more time: **they don't know what they don't know.** Don't feel guilty about talking to them or sharing these things with them. They need to know them, and you need to be the one who helps them with this. If appropriate, buy them a copy of the companion guide to this book, *Structuring Pastoral Compensation: A Practical Guide for Blessing Your Pastor*, to help them think through these same things we've talked about from the church's perspective.

And then, finally, commit all of this to the Lord. My goal has not been to make anyone discontent with what they have been given. Not every church or every pastor will be able to do everything written in this book the same way or to the same extent. Be thankful for what God has given you no matter what. I promise you – he's given you bread.

At the same time, reading this should not motivate you to pursue money as being some source of security in this world. Listen to the wisdom of Solomon (Proverbs 23:1-5):

> *1 When you sit down to eat with a ruler,*
> *observe carefully what is before you,*
> *2 and put a knife to your throat*
> *if you are given to appetite.*
> *3 Do not desire his delicacies,*
> *for they are deceptive food.*
> *4 Do not toil to acquire wealth;*
> *be discerning enough to desist.*
> *5 When your eyes light on it, it is gone,*
> *for suddenly it sprouts wings,*
> *flying like an eagle toward heaven.*

Did you notice what he said in verse 5? Wealth tends to sprout wings and fly away. You cannot put your trust in it. You cannot depend on it for either happiness or security.

The only thing you can depend on is the gracious, loving, and kind goodness of our Father who has promised to always give his children bread . . . no matter what. And it is into his hands that now I commit you, your church, and your finances knowing that he will always do for you exactly what is best.

APPENDICES

Appendix A
Form 4361 Explanation Letter

February 2, 2009

To the Elders of Cornerstone Bible Church,

This letter serves as my official notice (per the requirement of the Internal Revenue Service) that I have decided to file Form 4361 (Application for Exemption From Self-Employment Tax for Use by Ministers, Members of Religious Orders and Christian Science Practitioners).

Per IRS requirements, I certify that as a duly licensed minister (pastor/elder) of Cornerstone Bible Church, and because of religious principles, I am opposed to the acceptance (**for services I perform as a minister**) of any public insurance that makes payments in the event of death, disability, old age, or retirement; or that makes payments toward the cost of, or provides services for, medical care, including the benefits of any insurance system established by the Social Security Act.

The remainder of this letter will attempt to clarify and explain my decision.

Let me say that I have wrestled deeply with this question, and have not come to this conclusion lightly. My primary concern here is two-fold: 1) to be able to stand before God in honesty and integrity in this matter, and 2) to honestly evaluate my heart and my motives. Having sought counsel from Godly men, spent time in prayer, searched the Scriptures, and thought deeply about the many and complex issues involved, I have reached the conclusion stated above.

Many things have brought me to this conclusion.

First, the doctrinal statement of Cornerstone Bible Church clearly states:

> *We believe that every human being has direct relations with God, and is responsible to God alone in all matters of faith; that each Church is independent and must be free from interference by any ecclesiastical or political authority; that therefore Church and State must be kept separate as having different functions, each fulfilling its duties free from dictation or patronage of the other. However, we believe that the Church is to pray for, honor, and obey civil authorities except where to do so would violate plain commands and principles of the Word of God.*
>
> *I Timothy 2:5; Romans 14:7-9,12; Titus 3:1; Romans 13:1-7; 1 Peter 2:13-14*

Therefore, per our stated beliefs, with which I completely agree, as a minister of the Gospel, I am bound to follow the Scriptures in obedience and faithfulness.

This forces me to think through any Biblical material that may apply to the issue of paying the Self-Employment tax, and then receiving benefits from those payments.

Having studied through the Scriptures, two principles come together in my mind to form my decision. The first is a statement by Jesus that gripped my heart and gave me serious reason for reflection. The story is found in Matthew 22:15-21:

> *15 Then the Pharisees went and plotted how to entangle him in his words. 16 And they sent their disciples to him, along with the Herodians, saying, "Teacher, we know that you are true and teach the way of God truthfully, and you do not care about anyone's opinion, for you are not swayed by appearances. 17 Tell us, then, what you think. Is it lawful to pay taxes to Caesar, or not?" 18 But Jesus, aware of their malice, said, "Why put me to the test, you hypocrites? 19 Show me the coin for the tax." And they brought him a denarius. 20 And Jesus said to them, "Whose likeness and inscription is this?" 21 They said, "Caesar's." Then he said to them, "Therefore render to Caesar the things that are Caesar's, and to God the things that are God's."*

Two observations are worth noting here. First, Jesus very clearly supports the idea of general taxation and the believer's responsibility to honor that. There is no question about that. Second, He also very clearly draws a distinguishing line between the things that belong to Caesar (or the State) and the things that belong to God. The two do not mingle or overlap. The principle that I gain from this is the separation of things given to God and things given to the State. Each has its purpose and each must be honored.

The second principle of Scripture that has influenced my decision is the Biblical teaching on the support of a pastor/elder. A number of passages deal with this topic. I will begin with 1 Timothy 5:17-18, which says:

> *17 Let the elders who rule well be considered worthy of double honor, especially those who labor in preaching and teaching. 18 For the Scripture says, "You shall not muzzle an ox when it treads out the grain," and, "The laborer deserves his wages."*

Alexandar Strauch says, "According to Paul, all elders should be honored, but elders who rule well and work hard at preaching and teaching are entitled to 'double honor.' By using the expression, 'double honor,' Paul wisely avoids slighting other elders of their due honor and is able to call special attention to those who rule well and those who labor at teaching. So 'double honor' refers to honor for an elder of the church and honor for his extra labor."[49]

He then lists six reasons why the term 'honor' in this context is a reference to material aid (i.e. wages or payment for service).

First, he says, "Although the word 'honor' (timē) itself doesn't necessarily mean material assistance (2 Chron. 32:33; Prov. 26:1; Eph. 6:2; 1 Tim. 6:1), it includes in certain contexts the sense of material aid (Matt. 15:3-6; cf. Num. 22:17, 37; 24:11; Prov. 3:9; 14:31; 27:18; Dan. 11:38; Acts 28:10)."[50]

Second, "First Timothy 5:3 states, 'Honor widows who are widows indeed.' The 'widow indeed' is a truly destitute Christian widow. The

---

[49] Alexander Strauch, Biblical Eldership (Colorado Springs, CO: Lewis and Roth Publishers, 1995), 211.
[50] Strauch, 212.

instruction that follows (vv. 4-16) demonstrates that honoring these widows primarily involves monetary assistance (vv. 4,8,16). A church honors a destitute Christian widow by providing for her material livelihood."[51]

Third, "The biblical quotations in verse 18 show that material provision is uppermost in Paul's thought. The immediate context, therefore, indicates that 'honor' involves material maintenance."[52]

Fourth, "Using 'honor' rather than a more tangible term like 'money' is in harmony with Paul's choice of expression for financial matters. Paul favors terms that express grace, liberality, love, and partnership: service (Rom. 15:25,27; 2 Cor. 8:4; 9:1,12-13); fellowship (2 Cor. 8:4; Gal. 6:6; Phil. 1:5); grace (1 Cor. 16:3; 2 Cor. 8:6-7); liberality (2 Cor. 8-9); bounty (2 Cor. 8:20); blessing (2 Cor. 9:5); good work (2 Cor. 9:8); good things (Gal. 6:6); a fragrant aroma, an acceptable sacrifice (Phil. 4:18); seed (2 Cor. 9:10); harvest of your righteousness (2 Cor. 9:10); gift (Phil. 4:17); honor (1 Tim. 5:3,17)."[53]

Fifth, "The word 'honor' expresses financial compensation in a thoroughly Christian manner. Financial provision for elders is really honor due the elders, and such honor conveys the congregation's esteem, thoughtfulness, and loving concern."[54]

Finally, "The rights of some in the brotherhood to receive financial support is in full agreement with other passages of Scripture. Jesus was

---

[51] Strauch, 212.
[52] Strauch, 212.
[53] Strauch, 212-213.
[54] Strauch, 213.

a full-time teacher and preacher who was financially supported by the believing community (Luke 8:3). He called certain disciples to leave their employment and follow Him so that they could preach the gospel and teach believers (Luke 5:4-11; Matt. 28:19-20). Like their Master, they, too, depended on the loving financial support of others for their livelihood. Furthermore, Jesus taught that those who labor in the Word 'get their living from the gospel' (1 Cor. 9:14; Matt. 10:10). Paul also affirmed the right of those who preach and teach to receive financial provision from others (1 Cor. 9:4-14; 2 Cor. 11:8-9; Gal. 6:6; Phil. 4:16; 1 Thess. 2:5-6; 2 Thess. 3:8-9; Titus 3:13)."[55]

To support his statement in 1 Timothy 5:17, Paul quotes two Scriptures in verse 18. The first is Deuteronomy 25:4 – "You shall not muzzle an ox when it treads out the grain." "The context of Deuteronomy concerns equity and justice in daily life – even the right of an animal to enjoy the fruit of its labor while working for its owner."[56]

Paul explains and applies this passage from Deuteronomy and its connection to the support of pastors/elders in 1 Corinthians 9:6-14:

> *6 Or is it only Barnabas and I who have no right to refrain from working for a living? 7 Who serves as a soldier at his own expense? Who plants a vineyard without eating any of its fruit? Or who tends a flock without getting some of the milk?*
>
> *8 Do I say these things on human authority? Does not the Law say the same? 9 For it is written in the Law of Moses, "You shall not muzzle*

---

[55] Strauch, 213.
[56] Strauch, 214.

an ox when it treads out the grain." Is it for oxen that God is concerned? 10 Does he not certainly speak for our sake? It was written for our sake, because the plowman should plow in hope and the thresher thresh in hope of sharing in the crop. 11 If we have sown spiritual things among you, is it too much if we reap material things from you? 12 If others share this rightful claim on you, do not we even more?

Nevertheless, we have not made use of this right, but we endure anything rather than put an obstacle in the way of the gospel of Christ. 13 Do you not know that those who are employed in the temple service get their food from the temple, and those who serve at the altar share in the sacrificial offerings? 14 In the same way, the Lord commanded that those who proclaim the gospel should get their living by the gospel.

Strauch says, "To refuse to support hardworking teachers of the Word is as unjust, heartless, and selfish as muzzling an animal while it is working, which was a common practice among greedy, ancient farmers. The passage thus implies the provision of adequate living support, not merely token gifts, for the worker."[57]

The other Scriptural reference mentioned in 1 Timothy 5:18 comes from the lips of Jesus in Luke 10:7: "the laborer is worthy of his wages." As seen above in Paul's statement in 1 Corinthians 9:14, Paul understands and applies this comment to the support and care of those who labor in gospel ministry.

Other passages that teach this same principle are:

---

[57] Strauch, 214.

2 Corinthians 11:8-9 – 8 I robbed other churches by accepting support from them in order to serve you. 9 And when I was with you and was in need, I did not burden anyone, for the brothers who came from Macedonia supplied my need. So I refrained and will refrain from burdening you in any way.

Galatians 6:6 – 6 Let the one who is taught the word share all good things with the one who teaches.

Philippians 4:16 – 16 Even in Thessalonica you sent me help for my needs once and again.

1 Thessalonians 2:5-6 – 5 For we never came with words of flattery, as you know, nor with a pretext for greed—God is witness. 6 Nor did we seek glory from people, whether from you or from others, though we could have made demands as apostles of Christ.

2 Thessalonians 3:8-9 – 8 nor did we eat anyone's bread without paying for it, but with toil and labor we worked night and day, that we might not be a burden to any of you. 9 It was not because we do not have that right, but to give you in ourselves an example to imitate.

Titus 3:13 – 13 Do your best to speed Zenas the lawyer and Apollos on their way; see that they lack nothing.

And so, I believe the Bible is clear in its teaching on the support of those whose lives are given to the preaching and teaching of the Word of God. They must be supported by the church. It is a matter of obedience on the part of the congregation to support those elders whose lives are given to this task.

Naturally, a question now arises. How does the congregation do that? Well, in our situation, the congregation does that by giving offerings to God via the church. Money given to the church by the people is, in their minds and in actuality, money given to God. It is to be used for the needs of the church; or, as our church covenant clearly states, "to the support of the ministry, the expenses of the Church, the relief of the poor, and the spread of the Gospel through all nations."

My material aid (i.e. salary) is a direct result of people giving money to God via the church for the support of the ministry. This brings the two principles mentioned earlier together. First, as a minister of the Gospel, my support is to come from the people I serve, not the government. This distinguishes the payment of regular income taxes from the payment of any form of "public insurance." Regular income taxes go to support the workings and functions (I would even feel comfortable saying "ministry") of the government.

But "public insurance" is an entitlement program. Now, just to be clear and completely above board, I am not opposed (religiously speaking) to entitlement programs as a general principle. I may be opposed for personal reasons to particular entitlement programs, but as a general principle, I am not opposed to entitlement programs for religious reasons. I have spent over a dozen years in the secular workforce and have always paid my taxes and "public insurance" obligations without religious concern.

But the question before me now is a very specific one. Am I opposed to, based on religious principles, the acceptance of "public insurance" for my work in the ministry? Considering the fact that my support is commanded by God to come from the church, and considering the fact that money given to the church is money given to God, then I believe that my pay from the church for my work as a minister of the

Gospel should be exempt from "public insurance" obligations. The State has not been entrusted by God with the care of my family and I. The church has. And our church, in an act of obedience to God and love to me and my family, has chosen to bless us with material aid to meet our needs as we serve them. Therefore, I believe that it is wrong for that support to be diverted to the State for its use in supporting me and my family (thereby usurping – in some ways – the role of the congregation).

The State must not usurp the role of the church in providing for the elders of the church. Those funds were given by God's people to God's work in obedience to the Scriptures, and should not be diverted to any other institution or for any other purpose.

Again, let me be very clear. My desire in all of this is to provide a reasoned and Biblical mandate for a decision for which I (and I alone) am responsible. Other men will examine these same Scriptures and may come to differing conclusions.

For me, this entire quest began with a realization of a misunderstanding. After first becoming a pastor a little over a year ago, I was alerted to this issue. But, somehow, I misunderstood the question. I thought that the question at hand was whether or not I was opposed to the receipt of "public insurance" in general. As stated above. I am not. But recently, upon rereading the form, I recognized that the question was really whether or not I was opposed to receiving "public insurance" for my work as a minister. There is a large amount of difference in those two questions, and what I have sent to you for your understanding is the outworking of that realization.

In conclusion, I have had to search my heart and ask God to show me my own sinfulness. After studying these things, and spending time in prayer, and seeking counsel from Godly men, I have come to this conclusion, and I hope that my heart is as honest as I think it is. These issues in the Scriptures are real, and raise ethical questions in my mind that cannot be ignored. And so now, I give these things to God and place my trust in Him for all these things.

Sincerely,

Stacy Potts, Elder

APPENDIX B
NEXT STEPS

Here is a list of action items if you want to assess your pastoral compensation package:

1. Completely read *How to Not Be a Broke Pastor*.
2. What is your total current income (salary plus housing allowance)?
   _____
3. What is your current housing allowance designation?
   _____
4. What is your current salary (income minus housing allowance)?
   _____
5. Have you opted out of Social Security?
   _____
6. Are you still within the window of opting out of Social Security?
   _____
7. If so, what is the date by which you have to make a decision?
   _____
8. If you have not opted out of Social Security, how much is your actual net pay after SECA? _____
9. If you have not opted out of Social Security, how are your SECA payments being withheld? _____
   _____

10. How much does your church want you to net annually?
   _____
11. If you have not opted out of Social Security, how much would your church have to increase your salary in order for you to net this amount? _____
12. How does your church determine reasonable compensation for you? _____
   _____
13. Based on their method for determining reasonable compensation, is your current income reasonable? _____
14. Does your church offer you a parsonage? _____
15. If so, is the fair-market rental value of the parsonage being added to your total SECA calculation? _____
16. Would the church consider selling the parsonage? _____
17. Would you say that your church is treating its employees as well as, if not better than, the best secular employers around you? ___
18. Does your church provide medical insurance coverage for you?
   _____
19. If so, how much of the monthly premium does the church pay, and how much do you pay? _____
20. Describe the plan, its benefits, monthly premiums, copays, deductibles, and out-of-pocket maximum in as much detail as possible. _____
   _____
   _____
   _____
21. Have you read *Benefitting from Obamacare* to see how one church has saved over $100,000 in three years? _____

22. Does your church provide vision insurance coverage for you?
   _____

23. If so, how much of the monthly premium does the church pay, and how much do you pay? _____

24. Describe the plan, its benefits, monthly premiums, copays, deductibles, and out-of-pocket maximum in as much detail as possible. _____

   _____
   _____
   _____
   _____

25. Does your church provide dental insurance coverage for you?
   _____

26. If so, how much of the monthly premium does the church pay, and how much do you pay? _____

27. Describe the plan, its benefits, monthly premiums, copays, deductibles, and out-of-pocket maximum in as much detail as possible. _____

   _____
   _____
   _____
   _____

28. Does your church provide disability insurance coverage for you?
   _____

29. If so, how much of the monthly premium does the church pay, and how much do you pay? _____

30. Describe the plan, its benefits, and monthly premiums in as much detail as possible. _____

   _____
   _____

_____
_____
_____

31. How much paid time off do you receive annually? _____
_____
32. Have you ever been given a sabbatical? _____
33. Does your church offer a retirement plan for you? _____
34. If so, what type of plan is it? _____
35. Does the church contribute to this plan? _____
36. If so, how much is contributed on a monthly basis? _____
37. Have you bought a copy of *The Pastor's Guide to Wise Investing*?
_____
38. Does the church offer an accountable or non-accountable reimbursement plan for employees? _____
39. Is the plan written? _____
40. Describe the types of expenses that can be reimbursed. _____
_____
_____
_____
_____

41. Are these expenses fully reimbursed? _____
42. Does the church give bonuses/gifts to you? _____
43. From what funds do these bonuses/gifts come? _____
44. If collected through offerings or donations, are your donors informed that those funds are not tax-deductible? _____
45. Are bonuses/gifts added to your W2? _____
46. In total, do you think that your church is being as generous as it can be with its pastoral compensation package? _____

47. What needs are you facing right now? _____
_____
_____

48. Given the importance of the balance between a pastor's salary and housing allowance, have you considered the effect any changes made to your pastoral compensation may have on you? _____

49. How could your church improve your benefit package? _____
_____
_____

50. How could your church improve your retirement contributions?
_____
_____

51. Are there any reimbursements your church could add or increase?
_____
_____

52. Who is the church's attorney? _____
53. Who is the church's accountant? _____
54. Who is the church's tax professional? _____
55. Who is the church's financial planner? _____
56. When will you set up meetings with these four professionals to discuss any potential changes to your pastoral compensation package? _____
57. Have you bought a copy of *Structuring Pastoral Compensation* for every decision maker within your church? _____
58. Have you purchased a copy of *How to Not Be a Broke Pastor* for every pastor in your church? _____
59. Have you visited www.brokepastor.com for more insight into pastoral compensation issues? _____

60. Have you told other pastors you know about this book and website? _____

Visit www.brokepastor.com, the #1 online resource for understanding pastoral compensation and finance issues, for more topics, information, and resources that you can actually use.

Bless Your Pastor!

Is your church structuring its pastoral compensation package in a way that truly blesses your pastor? Is your church doing all it can and should to financially provide for the pastors who keep watch over your souls?

The fact of the matter is that most churches have never given any thought to what a pastoral compensation package should look like, and much less to how they should structure it so that their pastor receives the maximum benefit.

Structuring Pastoral Compensation is written for church decision makers (Elders, Deacons, Trustees, Committee Members, etc.) to help them understand what should be included in their pastor's compensation and how to best implement the various pieces so that their pastor will be truly blessed.

Could your church save **$100,000** or more?

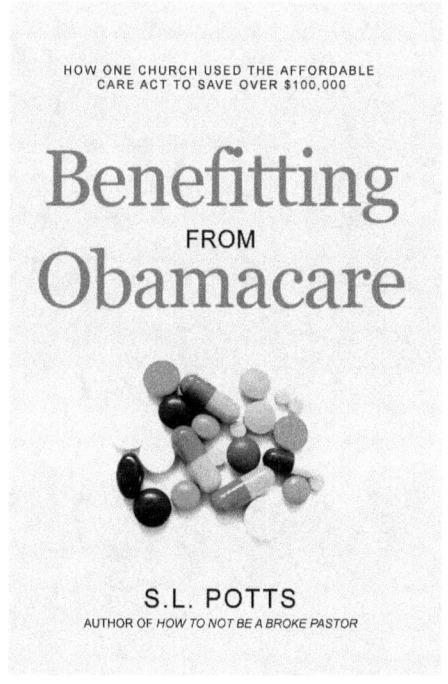

Over the past three years, our church has saved over $100,000 in health insurance premiums by using the provisions of the Affordable Care Act (a.k.a Obamacare) to our advantage - $100,000 that we have used to hire additional staff, send one of our members into foreign missions, and pay down our church's mortgage!

Written for both pastors and church decision makers, *Benefitting from Obamacare* is the story of how we did that, the challenges we faced, the things we had to consider, and what we have experienced since.

Learn to invest from the *Pros*!

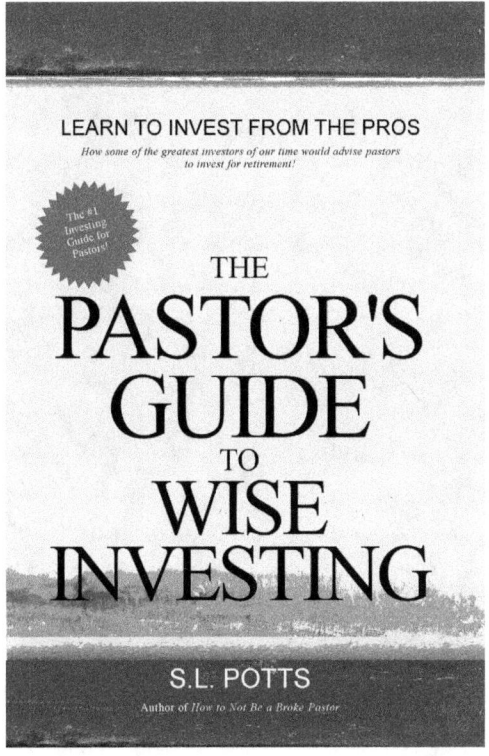

Pastors are so good at so many difficult things - preaching/teaching, counseling, discipling, caring - but can very often be completely clueless when it comes to handling their money wisely. This can be true of their day-to-day finances, but is often more true in regards to their retirement planning.

The Pastor's Guide to Wise Investing takes the, often, confusing world of investing and makes it simple and easy to understand by compiling and condensing the best advice from the best investors of our day into one simple, easy-to-read guide

www.ingramcontent.com/pod-product-compliance
Lightning Source LLC
LaVergne TN
LVHW051608070426
835507LV00021B/2837